Premier League

Liverpool F

ALEXANDER-ARNOLD
66
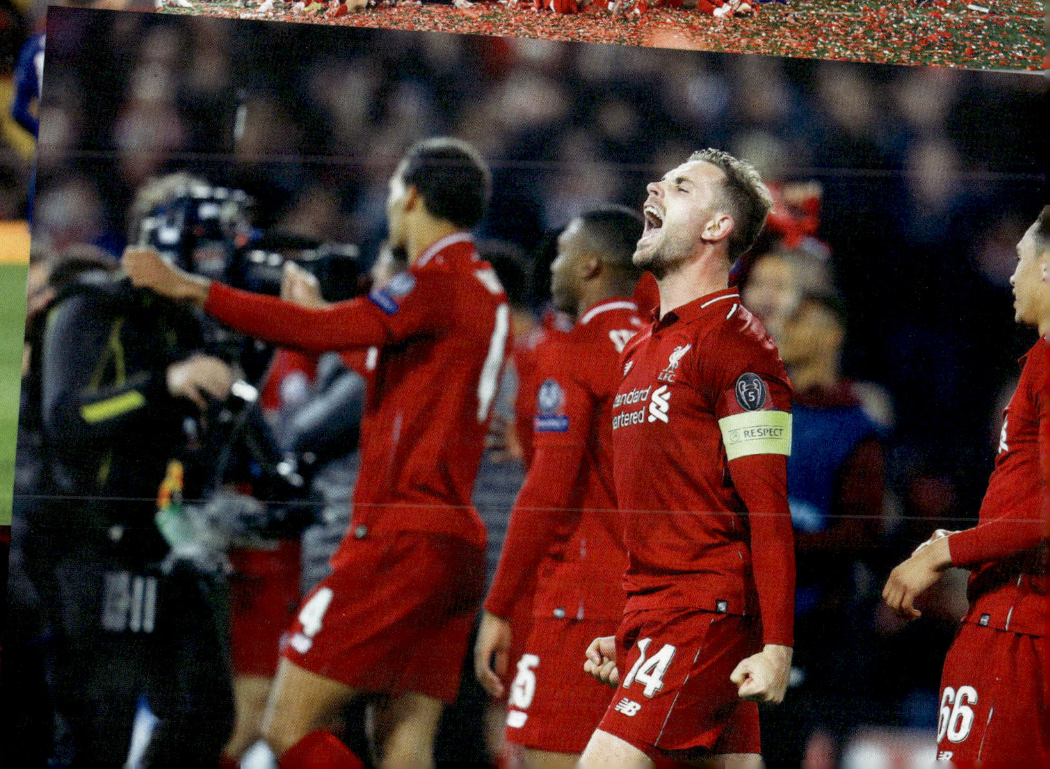

PAISLEY
LIVERPOOL
FOOTBALL CLUB

YOU'LL NEVER WALK ALONE 97
LEGEND
CHAMPIONS

# LIVERPOOL SCRAPBOOK

Written By
Michael O'Neill
with Iain Spragg

sona BOOKS

**First published in the UK by Danann Publishing Limited, 2020**
**Reprinted with corrections under the Sona Books imprint, 2025**



**CAT NO: SON0435**

Photography courtesy of The Press Association & Getty Images, Photoshot, UPPA, Talking Sport, Fotosports



Book layout and design: Darren Grice and Kevin Gardner
Project editor: Martin Corteel
Proof reader: Sofia Della Valle



**Printed in EU**
**ISBN: 978-1-912918-23-2**

# the CONTENTS

# THE FOOTBALL LEAGUE

Clubs dedicated solely to the sport of football were formed regularly throughout the 18th century. The London Gymnastic Society was one of the first created in the 1850s. The first club to be referred to as a club was the *"Foot-Ball Club of Edinburgh"* in Scotland in the period 1821 to 1824. Great Leicestershire Cricket and Football Club existed in 1840. The staff of Guy's Hospital in London formed Guys Hospital Football Club in 1843 which claims to be the oldest known football club, whilst Sheffield Football Club founded in 1857, is the oldest club documented as not being affiliated to a school, university or other institution. The oldest club still playing association football is Cambridge University Association Football Club.

Soon, club names that are recognisable to fans today were appearing; Bolton Wanderers (1874), Aston Villa (1874), Queen's Park (1867), Sheffield Wednesday (1867); and of course there was a certain Newton Heath LYR Football Club which was formed by railway workers in 1878. What would they say today about the extraordinary club they started?

The time had come to try and make a set of rules that would be adhered to by all the clubs. In 1862, thirteen London clubs met and hammered out regulations to govern the sport. This led to the formation of the Football Association in 1863 to oversee regulations for the sport.

No history of football would be complete if the name of Ebenezer Cobb Morley was not mentioned. He was a central figure in bringing the Football Association into being. He was a player himself and a founding member of the Football Association. As captain of his team, the Barnes Club, he proposed a governing body for the sport and so the meeting of the thirteen London clubs came about. From 1863-1866 he was the FA's first secretary and from 1867-1874 its second president. He drafted the *"London Rules"* at his home in Barnes in London.

EBENEZER COBB MORLEY

ORIGINAL HANDWRITTEN RULES 1863

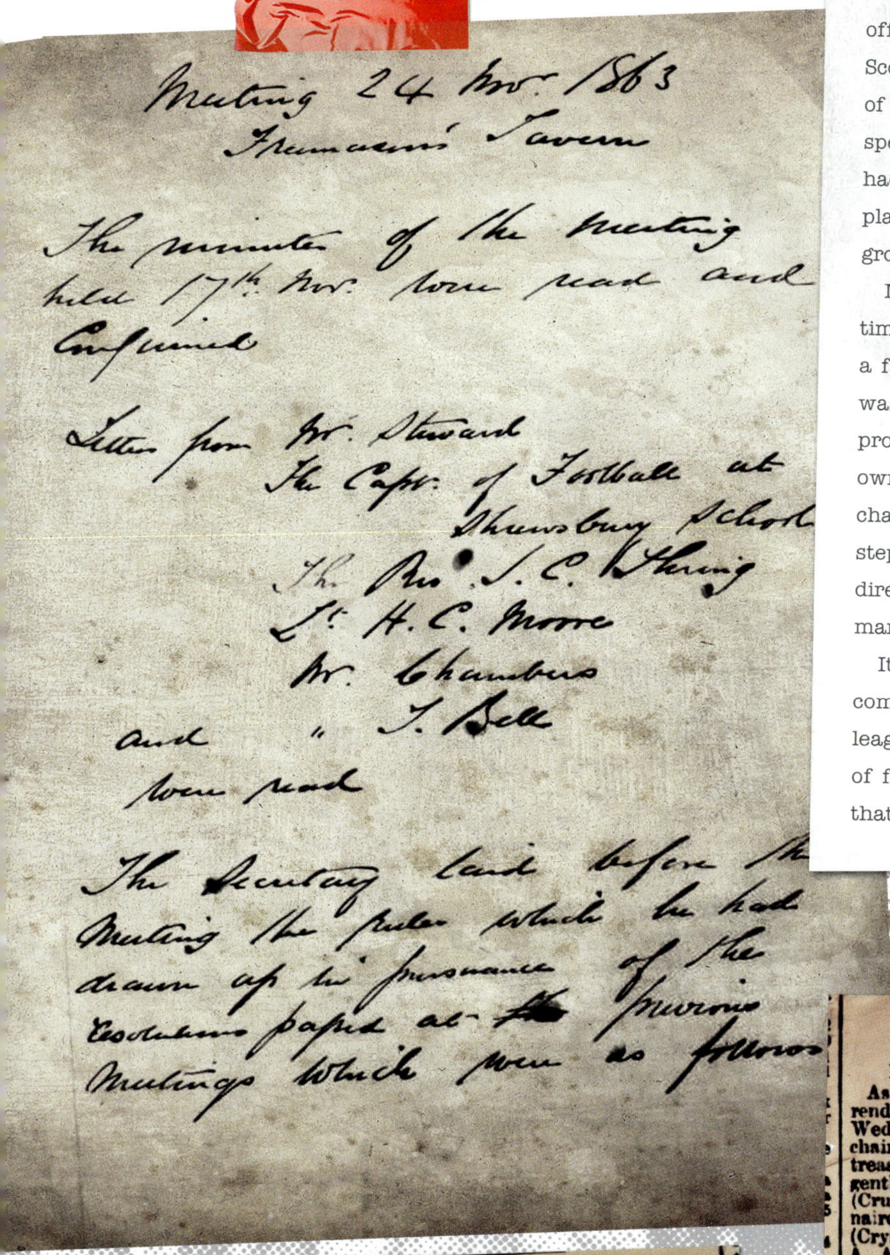

Meeting 24 Nov. 1863
Freemasons' Tavern

The minutes of the meeting held 17th Nov. were read and confirmed

Letters from Mr. Steward
The Capt. of Football at Shrewsbury School
The Rev. J. C. Thring
Lt. H. C. Moore
Mr. Chambers
and " J. Bell
were read

The Secretary laid before the Meeting the rules which he had drawn up in pursuance of the Resolutions passed at the previous Meetings which were as follows

Another event must be mentioned here: the first official, international game between England and Scotland took place in November 1872 on the West of Scotland cricket ground in Partick, Scotland. 4,000 spectators watched a 0-0 draw although the Scots had a goal disallowed. The very first game had taken place on the 5th March 1870 at the Oval cricket ground in London.

Most of the men playing in the teams at the time were amateurs, although betting had long been a feature of the sport. On the 18th July 1885 it was finally decided that football could become a professional sport. But clubs were still setting their own fixture dates and the whole structure was chaotic. Now was the moment for another man to step into the limelight, Mr. William McGregor, a director of Aston villa Football Club and to make his mark on history.

It was the 2nd March 1888. McGregor wrote to the committees of several football clubs to propose that a league competition would guarantee a certain number of fixtures and bring some order into the confusion that then existed. In Anderson's Hotel in London on

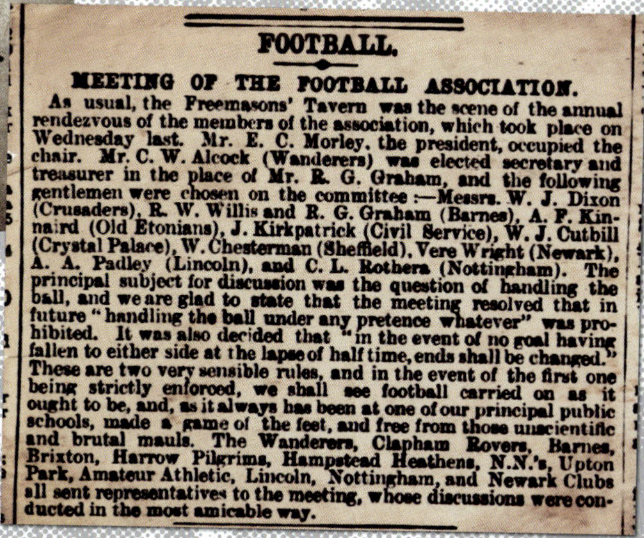

## FOOTBALL.

### MEETING OF THE FOOTBALL ASSOCIATION.

As usual, the Freemasons' Tavern was the scene of the annual rendezvous of the members of the association, which took place on Wednesday last. Mr. E. C. Morley, the president, occupied the chair. Mr. C. W. Alcock (Wanderers) was elected secretary and treasurer in the place of Mr. R. G. Graham, and the following gentlemen were chosen on the committee :—Messrs. W. J. Dixon (Crusaders), R. W. Willis and R. G. Graham (Barnes), A. F. Kinnaird (Old Etonians), J. Kirkpatrick (Civil Service), W. J. Cutbill (Crystal Palace), W. Chesterman (Sheffield), Vere Wright (Newark), A. A. Padley (Lincoln), and C. L. Rothera (Nottingham). The principal subject for discussion was the question of handling the ball, and we are glad to state that the meeting resolved that in future "handling the ball under any pretence whatever" was prohibited. It was also decided that "in the event of no goal having fallen to either side at the lapse of half time, ends shall be changed." These are two very sensible rules, and in the event of the first one being strictly enforced, we shall see football carried on as it ought to be, and, as it always has been at one of our principal public schools, made a game of the feet, and free from those unscientific and brutal mauls. The Wanderers, Clapham Rovers, Barnes, Brixton, Harrow Pilgrims, Hampstead Heathens, N.N.'s, Upton Park, Amateur Athletic, Lincoln, Nottingham, and Newark Clubs all sent representatives to the meeting, whose discussions were conducted in the most amicable way.

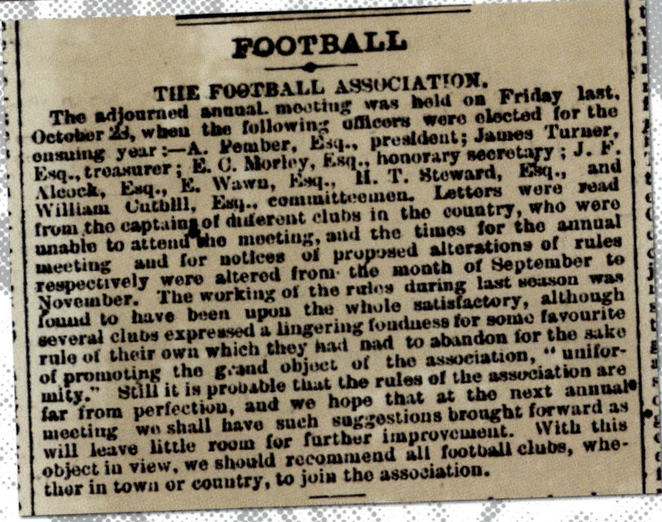

## FOOTBALL

### THE FOOTBALL ASSOCIATION.

The adjourned annual meeting was held on Friday last, October 23, when the following officers were elected for the ensuing year :—A. Pember, Esq., president; James Turner, Esq., treasurer; E. C. Morley, Esq., honorary secretary; J. F. Alcock, Esq., E. Wawn, Esq., H. T. Steward, Esq., and William Cutbill, Esq., committeemen. Letters were read from the captains of different clubs in the country, who were unable to attend the meeting, and the times for the annual meeting and for notices of proposed alterations of rules respectively were altered from the month of September to November. The working of the rules during last season was found to have been upon the whole satisfactory, although several clubs expressed a lingering fondness for some favourite rule of their own which they had had to abandon for the sake of promoting the grand object of the association, "uniformity." Still it is probable that the rules of the association are far from perfection, and we hope that at the next annual meeting we shall have such suggestions brought forward as will leave little room for further improvement. With this object in view, we should recommend all football clubs, whether in town or country, to join the association.

SPORTING LIFE 1870

SPORTING LIFE 1864

WILLIAM MCGREGOR REGARDED AS THE FOUNDER OF THE FOOTBALL LEAGUE

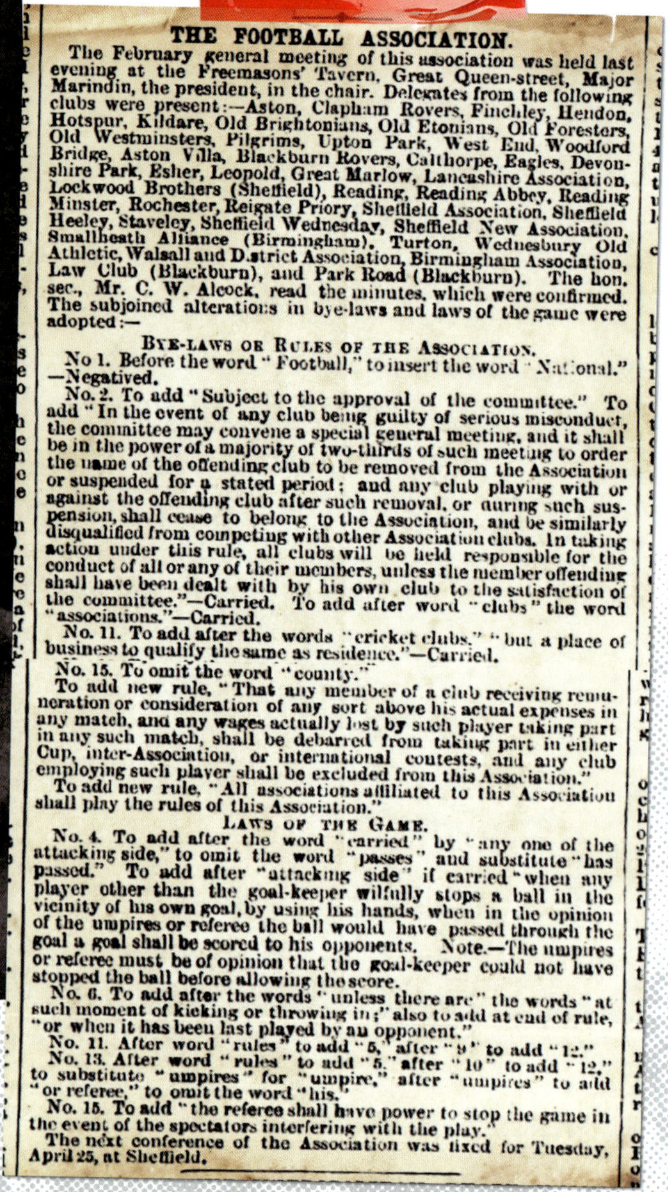

THE FOOTBALL ASSOCIATION.

The February general meeting of this association was held last evening at the Freemasons' Tavern, Great Queen-street, Major Marindin, the president, in the chair. Delegates from the following clubs were present:—Aston, Clapham Rovers, Finchley, Hendon, Hotspur, Kildare, Old Brightonians, Old Etonians, Old Foresters, Old Westminsters, Pilgrims, Upton Park, West End, Woodford Bridge, Aston Villa, Blackburn Rovers, Calthorpe, Eagles, Devonshire Park, Esher, Leopold, Great Marlow, Lancashire Association, Lockwood Brothers (Sheffield), Reading, Reading Abbey, Reading Minster, Rochester, Reigate Priory, Sheffield Association, Sheffield Heeley, Staveley, Sheffield Wednesday, Sheffield New Association, Smallheath Alliance (Birmingham), Turton, Wednesbury Old Athletic, Walsall and District Association, Birmingham Association, Law Club (Blackburn), and Park Road (Blackburn). The hon. sec., Mr. C. W. Alcock, read the minutes, which were confirmed. The subjoined alterations in bye-laws and laws of the game were adopted:—

BYE-LAWS OR RULES OF THE ASSOCIATION.

No 1. Before the word "Football," to insert the word "National."—Negatived.

No. 2. To add "Subject to the approval of the committee." To add "In the event of any club being guilty of serious misconduct, the committee may convene a special general meeting, and it shall be in the power of a majority of two-thirds of such meeting to order the name of the offending club to be removed from the Association or suspended for a stated period; and any club playing with or against the offending club after such removal, or during such suspension, shall cease to belong to the Association, and be similarly disqualified from competing with other Association clubs. In taking action under this rule, all clubs will be held responsible for the conduct of all or any of their members, unless the member offending shall have been dealt with by his own club to the satisfaction of the committee."—Carried. To add after word "clubs" the word "associations."—Carried.

No. 11. To add after the words "cricket clubs," "but a place of business to qualify the same as residence."—Carried.

No. 15. To omit the word "county."

To add new rule, "That any member of a club receiving remuneration or consideration of any sort above his actual expenses in any match, and any wages actually lost by such player taking part in any such match, shall be debarred from taking part in either Cup, inter-Association, or international contests, and any club employing such player shall be excluded from this Association."

To add new rule, "All associations affiliated to this Association shall play the rules of this Association."

LAWS OF THE GAME.

No. 4. To add after the word "carried" by "any one of the attacking side," to omit the word "passes" and substitute "has passed." To add after "attacking side" if carried "when any player other than the goal-keeper wilfully stops a ball in the vicinity of his own goal, by using his hands, when in the opinion of the umpires or referee the ball would have passed through the goal a goal shall be scored to his opponents. Note.—The umpires or referee must be of opinion that the goal-keeper could not have stopped the ball before allowing the score.

No. 6. To add after the words "unless there are" the words "at such moment of kicking or throwing in;" also to add at end of rule, "or when it has been last played by an opponent."

No. 11. After word "rules" to add "5," after "9" to add "12."

No. 13. After word "rules" to add "5," after "10" to add "12," to substitute "umpires" for "umpire," after "umpires" to add "or referee," to omit the word "his."

No. 15. To add "the referee shall have power to stop the game in the event of the spectators interfering with the play."

The next conference of the Association was fixed for Tuesday, April 25, at Sheffield.

SPORTING LIFE 1882

the 23rd March 1888, on the eve of the FA Cup Final, a meeting was held to discuss the proposal. Manchester was once again in the headlines when on the 17th April at the Royal Hotel, a final meeting created the Football League.

On the 8th September 1888, twelve clubs Accrington, Aston Villa, Blackburn Rovers, Derby County, Everton, Notts County, Preston North End, Stoke, FC., West Bromwich Albion and Wolverhampton Wanderers, sent their players out onto the turf for the first games in the new football league season.

Only once the season was underway was it decided that clubs would play against one another twice, once at home and once away, with two points awarded for a win and one for a draw. For the record, Preston won the first league title without losing a single game and won the FA Cup Final, too, the first league-FA Cup double.

Three clubs dominated during those first exciting years; Preston North End, Aston Villa and Sunderland; for fourteen seasons only three other clubs would win league titles; Everton, Sheffield United and Liverpool.

In 1892 the league expanded with the addition of a new Second Division. Liverpool, Arsenal and Newcastle United were now on the scene and a new name had been added to the First Division. A club with a glorious future had made its first steps to the top. Fourteen years had passed since they had first formed but now Newton Heath had arrived in the First Division.

Six years later, 1898, the number of clubs in each league had increased to eighteen and automatic promotion and relegation for two clubs was introduced the same year.

The Third Division was only added after WWI in 1921. By then another host of names that would later become legendary, including Tottenham Hotspur, Chelsea and Fulham, had been added to divisions that by 1905 had been boosted in numbers to 20 clubs in each. There were two third divisions in fact, the Third Division North and the Third Division South. Newton Heath by that time had become Manchester United having changed their name and moved to Old Trafford in 1902.

With the coming of WWII, the league was suspended for seven seasons. In 1950 there were 24 clubs in each of the two third divisions so there were now 92 league clubs. The third division clubs were amalgamated into a single division abolishing regionalisation and the Fourth Division was added in 1958. Four clubs could be promoted and relegated in the lower two divisions. In divisions one and two until 1974, two clubs made the climb or fell; the number was increased to three that same year.

The league now entered a period of calm with only minor changes such as altering the points system, three instead of two for a win introduced in 1981, and goal differences being taken into account. There was one enormous change ahead, however.

On May 27th 1992 the Premier League was formed. All First Division clubs resigned together from the Football League, which now operated with three divisions. The old system of interaction between the leagues, however, did not change but 104 years of tradition were over. The elite clubs were now, literally, in a league of their own. Money had tempted the top clubs and lucrative television rights deals beckoned them. The deal will soon be worth three billion pounds.

This wealth, of course, makes it almost impossible for a promoted club to compete with the big boys in the first season after promotion, and relegation often follows immediately. But the rewards for the successful are enormous with English Premier League clubs amongst the richest in the world and able to buy in players to make the....

## ....TERRACES ON A SATURDAY AFTERNOON ONE OF THE MOST THRILLING PLACES TO BE.

### THE FOOTBALL ASSOCIATION MEETING.

[FROM OUR OWN REPORTER.]

Last night the extraordinary general meeting, to reconsider the rejection of the amendment relating to law 5, proposed by the Clydesdale Club, of Glasgow, and supported by the Sheffield Association, was held in London at the Freemasons' Tavern, Major Marinder, the president, in the chair. The Scottish Association supported the new rule suggested by Mr. Kinnaird, of the Old Etonians, which was as under:—"When the ball is in touch a player of the opposite side to that which kicked it out shall throw it from the point on the boundary line where it left the ground in a direction at right angles with the boundary line at least six yards, and shall be in play when thrown in; the player throwing it in shall not play it until it has been played by another player." The Clydesdale amendment was as under, and was supported by Mr. Pierce Dix, the hon. secretary of the Sheffield Association; Mr. C. W. Alcock, hon. sec. of the Football Association, and others.—"When the ball is in touch, a player of the opposite side to that which kicked it out should throw it in from the point on the boundary line where it left the ground, in any direction the thrower may choose; the ball must be thrown at least six yards, and shall be in play when thrown in, but the player throwing it shall not play it until it has been played by another player."—The amendment was carried by 33 votes to 10, so that now London and Sheffield will have one code of rules.

SHEFFIELD DAILY TELEGRAPH 1877

# IN THE BEGINNING

The Liverpool story begins with the man who bought land at Anfield on which Everton FC could play their football matches. His name was John Houlding. Houlding had set up his own brewery in 1871 and ran it until he died in 1902.

He was a conservative councilor from 1894 becoming Lord Mayor of Liverpool in 1897-98. He was also president of Everton FC until the club committee removed him following a dispute about the Anfield ground. After this, Everton moved to Goodison Park to play.

Dislodged from Everton, Houlton was now the proud owner of a football ground but had no team to play on it. So he decided to form his own football club. The first rule of his club stated that the new club *". . . be called the Liverpool Football Club". It was formed on the 15th March 1892 at Houlding's home and with Houlding as president the "Liverpool Football Club and Athletic Grounds Company ltd"* was officially registered on 3rd June 1892.

Houlding gave Ulster man John McKenna the task of assembling the Liverpool team to play in the club's debut season. McKenna was known all over Liverpool for helping impoverished people in the town and his interest in the welfare of football players resulted in his becoming chairman of the Football League in 1910.

McKenna looked towards Scotland for players, which led to Liverpool being given the nickname of *"Team of the Macs." Two other Scotsmen, Duncan McLean and Tom Wyllie, left Everton to join the new club and Andrew Hannah came to the club from Renton to become the club captain. He was well known for his abilities in developing the talents of his team and his ". . . mature judgement, together with excellent defensive tactics . ."* made him an invaluable addition to the team according to the magazine Field Sports. The same magazine also praised not only the skills of winger Wyllie saying that he was as effective as any player in the country, but also his team mates.

JOHN HOULDING

An application to join the Football League was rejected and so Liverpool played their first games in the Lancashire League. Apparently someone had struck out the option to play in the Second Division in their application form and as the League did not want the club in the First Division they were denied entry to the League altogether.

On the 1st September 1892 the Liverpool FC team ran out onto the Anfield ground in their blue and

JOHN MCKENNA

white kit for a friendly match against Midland League side Rotherham Town to play their first match.

Two days later on the 3rd September 1892 Liverpool played their first Lancashire League game against Higher Walton at Anfield. It was a spectacular beginning with Liverpool winning 8-0. The first goal came from John Smith after 15 minutes and with Liverpool FC dominating the whole match the lads showed that they were a force to be reckoned with. The club could begin its legendary march to the top.

After this display, the crowd of 200 that watched their first game swelled to 4,000 for the second game. Liverpool disposed of the Lancashire Cup winners, Bury, 4-0. One man made his mark in this match, Scottish born John Miller. He would score 22 goals during this first season, scoring 5 goals when Liverpool defeated Fleetwood Rangers 7-0. Liverpool won 11 out of 13 league games and were challenging Blackpool for the title. At the end of the season it was Liverpool who took the League title on goal average over Blackpool. They had won the Lancashire League in their first season. It was an astounding start for the new team. But there was more glory to come.

On the 22nd April 1893, Liverpool ran out to compete in their first ever derby against Everton in the Liverpool Senior Cup final. Liverpool finished the game victorious, 1-0.

In 1893 the football league decided to increase the number of clubs. Once again, Liverpool was denied a place in the First Division. An unauthorised telegram was sent to the Football League by John McKenna, who received the reply, *"Liverpool elected. Come to London to decide fixture list tomorrow at 3 o'clock."* Liverpool were on their way. Both of their main goal scorers had left the club, however, so how would Liverpool fare against tough opposition?

The answer was very soon clear. In their first game of the season, Liverpool beat Middlesbrough Ironopolis 2-0. Joe McQue and Malcolm McVean scored the goals that began Liverpool's rise to the top of the Second Division undefeated in all their games. The club ended the 1893/94 season in first place, 8 points clear of Small Heath (who later became Birmingham city FC). In those years, promotion to the First Division was not automatic and a so-called test match had to be played against the bottom club of the First Division. That club was Newton Heath (who later became Manchester United). Liverpool took the lead halfway through the first half and never looked back winning 2-0 and gaining promotion to the First Division. Ten new players had made their debuts with Liverpool that season. One of them was 22-year-old James Stott who scored 14 goals making him top goalscorer.

In the FA Cup, Liverpool managed to beat mighty Preston North End, *"The Invincibles"* as they were known, 3-2, scoring after just 4 minutes. They lost to Bolton Wanderers in the 3rd round 3-0.

**THE LEGENDARY JIMMY ROSS CAME TO LIVERPOOL FROM PRESTON FOR THEIR FIRST SEASON IN THE FIRST DIVISION AND HE WENT ON TO SCORE 12 GOALS, SECOND ONLY TO THOMAS BRADSHAW WHO SCORED 18.**

# THE EARLY YEARS

Liverpool started the 1894/95 season with high hopes and when they met League champions Aston Villa in their third match of the season, the first at Anfield, it was watched by a record 20,000 people. With Liverpool leading 1-0 at half time it seemed that the world was at their feet. But Aston Villa scored twice in the second half to win the game. Liverpool never seemed to recover from this defeat and lost 3 out of their next 5 games. The praise turned to criticism and Houlding hoped that the derby with Everton could help the club turn the corner.

On the 13th October, Everton and Liverpool met for the first time in the First Division. 44,000 people turned out to watch highflying Everton beat Liverpool 3-0. Liverpool, it seemed, were not quite ready for the First Division.

In November Everton came to Anfield. It was an exciting game that ended in a 2-2 draw. Those who hoped that this performance would show a revived Liverpool team were disappointed. Although there were many goals the defence was weak resulting in 4 goal victories and 5 goal defeats. They were also knocked out of the FA Cup in the second round. When the season finished, Liverpool were at the bottom of the League. They would have to face a test match against Bury to stay in the division.

Five Liverpool regulars including David Hannah and Joe McQue were missing from the test match team. Liverpool lost 1-0 and were relegated to Division Two.

Houlding did not intend Liverpool to stay there. There were several signings of players so that the club could field a strong team in the 1895/96 season. Perhaps the most important of these was George Allen who came from Leith Athletic. In a dramatic season that would see Liverpool score a record 106 goals including a 10-1 victory against Rotherham, Allen scored 25 goals in 20 League games. Liverpool soared to the top of the Second Division. This time, however, there would be test matches against second-placed Manchester City, and Small Heath and West Bromwich Albion who were at the bottom of the First Division. Liverpool hammered in four against Small Heath keeping a clean sheet. The return match was a goalless draw. They then put two past West Bromwich Albion and with one game to go they had regained a position in the First Division.

**The question everyone was asking, of course, was could they stay there this time around?**

When John McKenna took up a position in the boardroom at the end of the season, Tom Watson, who was considered to be the best manager in the country, was persuaded to join Liverpool from Sunderland, a considerable feat of persuasion. Watson initiated a new regime at the club and the team was in training twice a day. And another change had taken place. When Liverpool ran out for their first game of the 1896/97 season against The Wednesday, they were wearing red shirts and white shorts. Now they would be nicknamed *"The Reds."*

LIVERPOOL SQUAD 1892-1893

Liverpool got off to a great start beating The Wednesday 2-1 only to lose their next two games. They also lost in their next derby game going down 2-1 to Everton. By November, however, the team had found their rhythm and emerged temporarily at the top of the First Division and even managed a 3-3 draw against League champions Aston Villa.

The New Year of 1897 also began auspiciously when Liverpool won four of their first five matches. But there was still inconsistency in their playing and this became obvious when they were thrashed 6-1 by Stoke City. In the FA Cup, they managed to reach the semi-final only to go down 3-0 against Aston Villa. Nonetheless, Tom Watson and his team had every reason to be confident for the future as they finished fifth in the League, a magnificent achievement. Once again, it was George Allen who put most goals past the opposition scoring 17 in all competitions. Unfortunately for *"The Reds"*, Allen left Anfield for Celtic in May 1897.

The first match of the new season in 1897/98 was against Everton on the 25th September. Liverpool had not beaten them for four and a half years and when Everton took the lead after twenty-three minutes, 30,000 spectators thought that another Everton win was beckoning. 7 minutes later Liverpool had equalised and before long they had taken the lead. A third goal in the second half gave Liverpool their first League victory over Everton. The inconsistency in their play, however, was still in evidence when they lost 3-0 to Everton 3 weeks later in a match more notable for physical attacks on players than exciting football. George Allen's departure had obviously made a difference and Liverpool finished the season in 9th position. Watson knew that he needed to bring in new blood to stop the slide.

On the 6th May 1898 19-year-old Alex Raisbeck was signed from Edinburgh Hibernians. Watson had made an inspired choice because the 19-year-old centre-half became a superstar in the club. His timing was superb and his athleticism helped him to conquer taller opponents. Watson also signed two more Scottish players, Tom Robertson and John Walker. Jack Cox, a clever, fast-paced winger had joined the team in December 1897. After a brief absence, George Allen also returned so Watson had a very strong team in place for the 1898/99 season.

This season, which was to prove to be their most exciting

ALEX RAISBECK 1896

so far, there were 18 teams in the First Division.

The Reds started in fine style beating The Wednesday 4-0 and Everton 2-1 before they fell victim to their inconsistency again losing three out of the next four games. By Christmas the fans were in despair only to see their team recover their form, score 10 goals and win 5 games out of 7 including another win over Everton, 2-0. Liverpool were also impressive in the FA Cup beating Newcastle 3-1 in the second round and West Bromwich Albion in the next round to bring them to the semi-finals and a match against Sheffield United. This round not only put paid to Liverpool's FA Cup hopes, it also did damage to their challenge for the League title.

Liverpool drew 2-2 in the first match and threw away a two-goal lead, twice, in the replay, which ended in a 4-4 draw. The second replay had to be abandoned when fans kept falling onto the pitch due to overcrowding in the stadium, and with Liverpool leading by one goal the game had to be abandoned; with it went Liverpool's FA Cup dream. In the next replay Sheffield United scored the only goal of the match and Liverpool's William Goldie was charged with *"discourteous language"* and banned for the remaining three matches of the season.

The Reds however, were challenging hard for the League title. They won 3 of their last 6 games and faced their main rivals Aston Villa in the final game with both teams on 43 points although Villa's goal average was better. Seemingly overwhelmed by the importance of the occasion Liverpool could do nothing to stop Aston Villa putting 5 goals past them by half time. That was the final score and Liverpool's League dream had died as well. There was, of course, great disappointment although Watson's team had proven that they had the quality to become future champions.

Yet as the club prepared to enter a new decade they were devastated by the death of the young man who had scored so many goals for them. George Allan was just 24 years old when he succumbed to tuberculosis and died on October the 16th 1899.

Perhaps his death hit the team more than might have been expected for at the start of the 1899/1900 season the spark had gone and the Reds lost eight matches in succession. No one could understand what had happened to the title challengers from last season.

It was clear that a replacement for Allan was not to be found amongst the present team and in January 1900 Sam Raybould was brought in from New Brighton Tower and Charles Satterthwaite was also signed up. The effect was immediate. Satterthwaite scored a hat trick in his second appearance. Raybould's first match was against West Bromwich Albion and he scored in his second appearance. The team began to pull together and after winning eight of their last ten games they were at least in tenth position when the season ended.

So there was reason for optimism when they ran out for the first match of the 1900/01 season and even more at the end of the first game against Blackburn when they emerged as 3-0 victors. Perhaps the see-saw ride would now be over. Ten goals in three games had the fans cheering as did a 1-1 draw against Everton before a wobble caused three lost games out of the next six. But then hopes of great things in store rose after a 5-1 thrashing of champions Aston Villa.

Then they lost impetus again. It seemed as though the old problem of inconsistent form was going to deny them glory once more. They lost the next two games as well,

ARTHUR GODDARD 1903

which saw the end of their FA Cup challenge. As February came around and a match against the powerhouse Sunderland, there was little to cheer about. And then the miracle happened. Perhaps Liverpool was inspired to check mate Tom Watson's old club. But when they finished the afternoon 1-0 winners they began to pick up speed again. 5 wins and three draws in the next eight games with 13 goals to their credit and the Reds were back in the title race. With 2 games left to play Liverpool had 41 points to Sunderland's 43. Sunderland had played all their games.

Nottingham Forest was first up and Liverpool showed what they were capable of under pressure, winning 2-0. Now everything depended on one match against West Bromwich Albion. Liverpool kept their fans on tenterhooks, and goals were almost scored at both ends until finally Walker hit the back of the net for Liverpool. The whistle went and the Reds had made it. The League title was theirs at last!

Watson could not bring the sparkle back for the 1901/02 season and Liverpool found themselves unable to struggle out of the lower regions of the League. One of a few high points that year was the 7-0 drubbing of Stoke in January in which Andy McGuigan scored 5 goals, the second Liverpool player to do so. John Miller had been the first.

The man who was later to become a Liverpool legend, Arthur Goddard arrived in February, too, but was unable to prevent the Reds from dropping to eleventh place at the end of the year. It was baffling and disappointing. But the death of the man whose dream had brought the club into being saddened everyone. John Houlding had lived long enough to see his hopes fulfilled and his team win the League title. He died in France on the 17th March 1902.

Liverpool were able to recover some of their previous form in the 1902/03 season with Raybould hammering home 32 goals in 34 appearances, the first man to score 30 goals in one season for the club. His talents could not take Liverpool higher than fifth that season but what happened next was unbelievable.

Liverpool started the 1903/04 season with five losses in five games. Raybould along with Glover and Goldie were banned for accepting what amounted to bribes to join Portsmouth and were banned from playing until the new year of 1904. Liverpool could not recover from the loss of three key players. They dropped down the table to within sight of relegation, which was now automatic for the last two teams. Of the three banned players only Raybould returned but he did not perform as he had in the past. Winning just nine games Liverpool ended the season second from the bottom and were relegated. Everyone looked for

LIVERPOOL F.C. 1905-1906, THE FIRST DIVISION LEAGUE CHAMPIONS

an answer to end this constant up and down form.

Losing the first game of the 1904/05 season 2-0 in the Second Division was not what anyone wanted. But help was at hand because there was a new star about to rise that no one had predicted. Jack Parkinson hit 20 goals in 21 games that season scoring more than Boulding and Robbie Robinson. After the sticky start, the Reds began to bring in the results that mattered. The defence was playing well, too, with Raisbeck hitting top form. They became unstoppable and showed the other title contenders who was going to win this season with a 1-1 draw against Bolton and a 4-0 win against Manchester United. They finished top of the table and were back in the First Division.

It was true to form then, when the Reds lost their first three matches in the 1905/06 season, the last a terrible 5-0 drubbing at the hands of Aston Villa. And the Reds continued to bounce unsteadily along for the games that followed. They were victorious against Sunderland when Raybould struck twice but lost to Everton before beating Derby by an impressive 4-1 and losing to The Wednesday 3-2. When Sam Hardy joined the club as goalkeeper their form stabilised. Hardy was one of the best keepers of his day. Liverpool began to notch up the victories, 4-1 against Nottingham Forest, Middlesbrough 5-1 Newcastle 3-2 Aston Villa the League leaders were hammered with 3-0 at Anfield with Hardy on top form saving a penalty. The Reds won 11 out of 14 games and went to the top of the table. The FA Cup dream vanished again this season when they were beaten by Southampton but in the League, Liverpool were proving their mettle. 3-0 against Newcastle, 1-1 against Everton, 2-0 against Wolves. They finished their season as League champions with a 3-1 win against Sheffield United. To add a little shine to the already successful year, Liverpool beat Corinthians 5-1 in the Sheriff of London Charity Shield in which the best amateur teams played the best professional side.

Having taken his team to two League titles Watson wanted a stand that befitted his team. Another legend was about to rise. A new grandstand was planned, to be in place for the 1907/08 season but for the coming season new concrete terracing was built by Walton Breck Road. It was Ernest Edwards the Sports editor of the Post and Echo who called the terrace *"Spion Kop". This referred to the men who died during a Boer War battle in southern Africa on the 24th January 1900 to capture a hill known as "Spioenkop", "Spy Hill."* The famous Kop was born, 100 steps rising up 50 feet. The finished ground would be able to house 60,000 spectators.

The new season of 1906/07 got under way on the 1st September with a 1-0 win against Stoke. So that was alright. Except that nothing was right. There followed two draws and then five successive losses. The old spectre of inconsistent form raised its head again. This was proven when the lads then went on to a winning streak with

EVERTON & LIVERPOO
OFFICIAL
Football Programme
The only Programme published by Authority of the Everton & Liverpool C
1909-10.
Vol. 6—No. 34 (Copyright, Entered at Stationers' Hall.) SATURDAY JAN. 29, 1910. PRICE
SIXTH YEAR
Great Concession. During January onl
Suits to Measure
26/6
7/6 Trousers 7/6
First-rate Materials
Sound Workmanship
Excellent Trimmings
and an Assured Fit
The Whole Stock shown in the Windows
ONE PRICE ONLY
BEATY BROS. Ltd.
The Celebrate
Tailors
ONLY Addresses } London Road and Church Street, LIVERPOO
ROYAL HIPPODROME, TWICE NIGHTLY AT 6-50 AN

seven of the next nine matches going in their favour. Once they had been presented with their winners' medals for the previous season they scored not a single goal in the next five matches. Criticism of the team began to grow loud. What was wrong when they could win a championship one year and then crash the next?

The match against Sunderland seemed to symbolise this see-saw effect in the team's achievements. 4-1 up at half time with great football played they withered in the second half to allow Sunderland to depart with a 5-5 draw. A sparkling win against Newcastle 4-1 was the precursor to five losses in eight games. It was like a curse. Relegation loomed close by and was only just avoided when the Reds ended this ragged season in fifteenth place.

Sam Raybould left at the end of the season, which was a blow to the struggling team who would sorely miss his goalscoring skills. Liverpool began the 1907/08 season without Raisbeck who was ill and lost their first game 3-1 to Nottingham Forest. Manchester United then walloped them 4-0 leaving them bottom of the table. Fortunately Raibeck returned before the damage was too great and Liverpool won two out of the next three games with one drawn. They beat Everton 4-2 with Raisbeck scoring a brilliant goal and when the Reds sank Sunderland 1-0 the fans became more cheerful about the team's prospects. Except that Raisbeck had now been injured and could not play for two months.

Liverpool still could not produce consistently good football. They could win 6-0 at Notts County only to lose three times in a row and get knocked out of the FA Cup again to Newcastle having been one up at half time. Then they thrashed Manchester United 7-4 to finish in eighth place. Safe, at least.

The League decided that the £4 wage limit was to be abolished this season and the way was open for the stars of the game to reap the benefits. Liverpool players, so it seemed in the later months of the 1908/09 season, would not profit; they were soon once more in danger of dropping out of the Division altogether. Two 5-0 defeats brought them to their lowest ebb. At the end of the season, needing one point to avoid relegation, they had to face Newcastle, who already had the League title in their pockets. Ronald Orr saved Liverpool's blushes and his goal was enough to secure victory for the Reds and another season of First Division football.

It was obvious that changes needed to be made. Three men moved on; Alex Raisbeck the greatest player the club had seen, Jack Cox and Maurice Parry. John McKenna moved from vice-chairman to Chairman. Two Scotsmen, James Stewart and John McDonald arrived and the Reds went into intense training in the closed season.

DONALD MCKINLAY 1910

At the start of the 1909/10 season Liverpool got down to business and won eight out their first ten games and dispensed with Everton and Manchester United along the way. They were strong in attack and had a good defence. There was an historic match against Newcastle in December when Liverpool seemed in for a thrashing as they were 5-2 down at half time. Suddenly galvanised, Liverpool produced astonishing football to pull the game back and win 6-5. Chelsea and Arsenal fell before the red onslaught. With a run of good results the Liverpool team managed a two-goal victory over Aston Villa who were already champions by that time, to secure a second place. Jack Parkinson had become the star striker with 30 goals to his credit and an England selection to look forward to. So there was reason to be optimistic.

Yet once again Liverpool could not follow up success with success. The game of snakes and ladders continued and in the 1910/11 season they lost seven of their first ten games. Keeper Hardy had a wrist injury that kept him from playing. Liverpool could not move up the table.

ELISHA SCOTT 1912

Newcastle hammered them 6-1 and they were kicked out of the Cup by Everton. They only managed 13th at the end of the season. There was worse to come.

The Reds could only gel properly sporadically and slipped even further down the table in the 1911/12 season. Two draws and a defeat got their games underway and they continued to struggle for the rest of the season. Fulham knocked them out of the FA Cup and Sam Hardy had to be replaced by an inexperienced 19-year-old, Kenneth Campbell. Liverpool had to draw their final game against Oldham in order to stay in the First Division. Two minutes into the game Samuel Gilligan scored Liverpool's winner. The team had scraped home for another year with fifteenth place.

After 240 games, Hardy had played his last match for Liverpool and was sold to Aston Villa. Liverpool continued on their mediocre path in the 1912/13 season, too. Although they started off well enough with three successive wins, a run of six defeats did great damage to their position in the table. They were able to beat Everton 2-0 but were crushed by a Sunderland team that put 7 goals past them at Roker Park and beat them 5-2 at Anfield. Newcastle put them out of the Cup and they ended the year on 12th place. The following season 1913/14 had even less League comfort for the fans and a 14th place was all the Reds could manage.

There was, however, a great Cup run to stir the fans' hearts. Liverpool made it to the final for the first time in their history with an unexpected win over Aston Villa. In a hard match, Liverpool came away 2-0 winners to meet Burnley in the final. It was not the most exciting game and Burnley came away with a 1-0 victory that they deserved.

That year, war was declared but as everyone assumed that it would be over by Christmas a new League season was scheduled. Liverpool, however, were now firmly wedged in at the bottom of the League and landed on 16th place in the 1914/15 season.

By then it was clear that the war was not going to be a short one and the League and Cup games were suspended, with only regional games played from then on. Many footballers signed up to fight. The Footballer Battalion was the nickname for the 17th Service Battalion of the Middlesex Regiment as its core was made up of footballers. The battalion fought at the Somme amongst other battles.

That year Tom Watson died on the 6th May. He remains the longest serving manager at the club with 742 matches being played when he was in charge. He was just 56 years old.

* * * *

The League started up again for the 1919/20 season with players such as Jackie Sheldon, Walter Wadsworth and Bill Lacey who was now 30, back in the team. There were new signings, Ephraim Longworth from Leyton and Tom Bromilow amongst others.

And young players before the war such as Donald Mackinlay now shone in the post-war game. Elisha Scott would soon become one of Liverpool's greatest goalkeepers. Longworth and Mackinlay played alongside one another for 18 years, a League record for full-backs. It was also time for a new manager to take over the reigns and on the 17th December 1919, David Ashworth agreed to come to Liverpool from Stockport County.

Before Ashworth arrived, Liverpool looked patchy on the field. When he took over he steadied the players and the results began to improve. He gave the Kop the joyous sight of Liverpool beating Everton for the first time since 1899. Harry Lewis hit the first for Liverpool after just five minutes with Tom Miller, a player active before the war, scoring two more for the Reds.

Now the team was in full flow and eight games in succession brought 18 goals and a clean sheet. There was a good FA Cup run, too, which Huddersfield brought to an end in the fourth round 2-1 and Liverpool could be pleased that they landed on fourth place that year. Now they would have to consolidate their position.

That year, the League expanded to 66 clubs when the Southern Division was amalgamated to become the Third Division making the League national at last.

Liverpool entered the 1920/21 season in buoyant spirits. 12 games without defeat showed the other teams that Liverpool meant business. There was a 6-0 thrashing of Preston North End and enormous joy when Everton were beaten home and away going down 1-0 at Anfield and 3-0 at Goodison Park. By all accounts this latter match was a cracker and started off at high speed with the football full of artistry and skill. Liverpool went ahead after fifteen minutes through an ingenious Johnson goal from a seemingly impossible position. Chambers scored the next two for an historic win for the Reds. Chambers got his first England cap later in the season.

A 1-0 defeat to Bradford came as a cold shower and brought an anxious wait to see if this was a bad omen. It was, as Liverpool then suffered three defeats to leave themselves adrift on 4th place at the end of the season, disappointing after showing so much promise.

For Jackie Sheldon the season was his last in football. When Liverpool played Derby on the 16th April 1921, Sheldon was caught in a tackle and his leg broken so badly that he was never able to play again. A sad end, especially as he missed one of the most exciting season's in the club's history.

In their typical way, Liverpool lost their opening match of the 1921/22 season 3-0 to Sunderland only to begin a run of 14 games without defeat. Goals were proving hard to come by, however. Nonetheless, a terrific 4-0 win over Middlesbrough landed the Reds on top of the League on the 19th November. Harry Chambers scored three goals in an undefeated Christmas season and Liverpool went into the new year with good hopes. They were not to be disappointed.

Sunderland were dispatched from the FA Cup in a great 5-0 win and Liverpool followed up with three wins in the League. The defence was playing well; they kept the ball out of the Liverpool net for five successive games, before a familiar disease struck the team. They lost to Bolton and Arsenal and were hammered by Oldham 4-0 the worst defeat of the season.

The race for the title suddenly opened up. There were

four games to go when reigning champions Burnley came to Anfield on the 17th April. With 53 points, the Reds were heading the table. If Tottenham Hotspur lost then a win would make the Liverpool side unassailable. Liverpool obliged by winning 2-1 and Oldham ditched Tottenham's hopes 1-0. Liverpool had made it by six points and seen rivals Manchester United relegated. After 16 years, the Reds had won the League title again.

Ashworth decided to leave the team practically unchanged during the summer. But there was to be a bizarre change of personnel when the 1922/23 season was already well under way.

Liverpool came out fighting into the new season beating Arsenal 5-2 with Dick Johnson nabbing a hat-trick. They collapsed again to lose the next two games against Arsenal and Sunderland before they regained their confidence with a 5-1 revenge defeat of Sunderland that included a mighty Harry Chambers shot that punctured the ball. Chambers would go on to net a total of 25 goals that season as Liverpool's highest goalscorer.

There were also two victories against Everton again this year to warm supporters' hearts, the first game producing a 5-1 win for the Reds. By the middle of December Liverpool were on top of the table and heading for a second title when the bombshell dropped. David Ashworth decided to leave the club and return to Oldham before Christmas. There were family reasons it seemed as his wife and daughter were both invalids and he wanted to be closer to them. But with Liverpool riding high it was terrible timing.

Fortunately the departure did nothing to strangle the Liverpool charge and by the 13th February there was a new man at the helm; Mattie McQueen. The FA Cup eluded the Reds again this season; they were knocked out by

PLAYERS IN ACTION DURING AN FA CUP MATCH BETWEEN ARSENAL AND LIVERPOOL JANUARY 1923

Sheffield United as they had been twice before.

By April of 1923 Liverpool were still on top of the table separated by four points from Sunderland. There was an anxious wait when the Reds drew 1-1 against Huddersfield but Sunderland lost 2-0 to Burnley and the Liverpool team had done it again. They had become just the fifth side to win the title twice in succession since the League had been formed in 1888. A wonderful achievement.

Who could have imagined that for Liverpool, filled with such high hopes for the future, that year was to be the pinnacle of their achievements until the end of the Second World War?

The 1923/24 season began as a new season so often did, with a defeat. 0-2 against West Bromwich Albion and then a mighty trouncing of Birmingham City 6-2 so all seemed to be well. But instability had crept back into the players' performances and in November, when full back Jock McNab was injured and manager Matt McQueen was hit by a taxi and his leg amputated, the warning signs were flashing. Liverpool were losing their grip on the League and had lost 11 matches by the end of the year. Newcastle put paid to their Cup hopes winning 1-0 in a bad-tempered match that saw both Wadsworth and McNab sent off. Liverpool fell to 12th place by the end of the season.

When the South African team visited and beat Liverpool in a friendly in October, two of the African players, Arthur Riley and Gordon Hodgson made such an impression that they were signed up for Liverpool for the 1925/26 season. Hodgson made his debut in December 1925.

Liverpool were able to get back up to 4th place by the end of the following season, 1924/25 although it started off with three losses from the first four matches. Dick Forshaw was leading goalscorer with 19 in all competitions. And the most notable aspect of the 1925/26 season apart from Forshaw's 19 goals, was the arrival of Gordon Hodgson in December 1925, who became a menace to every opposition goalkeeper from that time on. Despite Liverpool hammering 5 past both Manchester United and Everton, they slipped back from the previous year's 4th, to finish in 7th position.

The 1926/27 season was no more successful with Liverpool in the relegation zone at one point. Hodgson caught pneumonia in December and was absent from the team for two and a half months. The Reds missed him badly and did not recover their form, losing 11 games out of 24. In March 1927 Dick Forshaw was sold to Everton. It was not form that precipitated the sale but lack of funds in the club's coffers. Forshaw's departure did not please the fans. He had been a vital cog in the team despite his 31 years.

Another vital player would leave Anfield in the 1927/28 season. After a career that had spanned 339 games and with 151 goals to his credit, Harry *"Smiler"* Chambers left Liverpool in March 1928. He was 31 years old. He was followed by Ephraim Longworth at the end of the season who had played 370 games. By then Liverpool had ended the season on 16th place with just 39 points, 1 point clear of relegation.

As the team headed into the 1928/29 season the club knew that they had a fight on their hands to remain in the First Division. The team fought its way back to 5th position and the supporters were rewarded with a new stand. The Kop was given a roof to provide shelter for 28,000 fans and linked to the two main stands and its formal opening took place on the 25th August 1928.

Another event that took place that year was the retirement of Donald Mackinlay at the age of 38. Over 18 years at the club, he had enjoyed one of the longest careers of any Liverpool player having made his debut at 19 years of age in 1910.

A new decade was around the corner and everyone was anxious to end the uncertainty that had plagued the results for many years. But the 1929/30 season showed the team was still unable to pull itself to the top of the division. Even though they managed to get themselves into 4th place at one stage, they hit a bad patch and lost 5 out of 6 games scoring just 3 goals. So they started the new decade by finishing in 12th place.

As the decade continued, the fans would find themselves wishing that the team could reach that position again.

Despite Hodgson scoring a record 36 League goals in the 1930/31 season, the team seemed unable to capitalise on his talents finishing in 11th place, and in 10th place the following season despite starting well and another 26 goals from Hodgson. Bolton Wanderers hit 8 past the Reds in the disastrous 8-1 final game of the season. Even the Cup run that brought them to the quarter-finals ended in defeat at the hands of a club that was below them in the League. They lost to Chelsea 2-0.

Gordon Hodgson was doing his best to bring about a change in the club's fortunes. He was top goalscorer again in the 1932/33 season with 24 goals but it was a losing lone battle that even a 7-4 victory over Everton could not alter. The mediocre team form continued and was rewarded with 14th place as the season ended.

But there was an even worse season ahead that saw the Reds win just one of their first 6 games. There was a run of 12 games without a win and a 9-2 humiliation at the hands of Newcastle and as their season staggered to a close Liverpool were down fighting for survival in the Division. They finished 18th, just 2 points away from danger. Neither were the supporter's best pleased to find that one of their idols, keeper Elisha Scott was going to be transferred. For many, not just Liverpool supporters, he was the best goalkeeper of all time.

In an effort to strengthen the defence, Tom Cooper, who was one of the best full backs in the country, joined Liverpool for the 1934/35 season. It did little good, for the Reds conceded 8 against Arsenal in the third match and another 8 against Huddersfield even though they were still capable of hammering 5 past Stoke and 6 past Chelsea. Astonishingly they were on 7th place when the season ended.

By now the fans were accustomed to the snakes and ladders seasons at Anfield. Which was just as well?

In 1935/36 the Reds would once again be fighting relegation and see the departure of their star forward, Gordon Hodgson.

There were moments of brilliance as usual. On the 7th September Everton came to Anfield. Liverpool wiped the floor with their rivals slamming in 6 goals in a 6-0 victory. Then came the inevitable crash, a 6-0 defeat against Manchester City followed by another terrific performance when they won 7-2 against Grimsby Town. But these wins were cold comfort for landing in 19th place. 1936 brought the news of the death of John McKenna at the age of 82. Mckenna had been vital in Liverpool's history and his importance to the football world in general was widely recognised.

Liverpool acquired a new manager before the 1936/37 season; 44-year-old George Kay. His appearance changed nothing and for the second season in succession, Liverpool were fighting relegation. They lost 7 games in a row mid-season and as the season dragged to its close, they conceded 5 goals in each of two defeats against Manchester City and 4 in each of another two defeats. No one could have been surprised by the 18th final place.

It was far more surprising to finish the season of 1937/38 in 11th place especially after crashing 6-1 to Chelsea in the first game of the season. The Reds managed

to restrict the number of games in which they conceded 5 goals, to a single match against West Bromwich Albion in 1938 when they lost 5-1. Even more surprising was that they managed to get to 11th place with their top goalscorer, Alf Hanson, netting just 14 goals. A certain Matt Busby made 33 League appearances for the club that season.

Then Liverpool repeated the trick in the 1938/39 season with top goalscorer Berry Nieuwenhuys also scoring 14 goals. For the record, Matt Busby scored once that season which was only conspicuous because of the statistics that delivered 14 wins, 14 draws and 14 defeats, a result symbolic of Liverpool's form throughout the decade.

Then, after Liverpool had got off to a good start and won two of their first three games the next season, another war came along. The League suspended all matches and the Liverpool men kept their skills intact by joining the Western League. One man who played his one and only match for Liverpool...

**...ON MAY 30TH 1942 WAS A CERTAIN BILL SHANKLY. MORE ABOUT HIM LATER.**

# THE POST WAR YEARS

The League resumed games for the 1946/47 season and the Liverpool side looked very different from the one that had played before the war started. Jack Balmer, Berry Nieuwenhuys, Willie Fagan and Phil Taylor ran out into the new season as they had in 1938/39. Albert Stubbins joined the Reds in September and his presence was immediately felt. He became top goalscorer alongside Jack Balmer with 24 goals that season.

Liverpool began in what had almost become the traditional way with a win and a loss. And then came a match that heralded the way forward and went down in Kop history as one of the most exhilarating matches ever played.

Liverpool met Chelsea on September 7th 1946. Bob Paisley and Billy Liddell were in the side and Liddell got the first goal after just two minutes. The floodgates opened for Liverpool and Bill Jones scored two in six minutes with Willy Fagan getting a fourth for the Reds. It seemed to be all over for Chelsea especially when Balmer netted a fifth just after half time. A sixth goal in the 50th minute by Liddell was a bonus. On fifty-five minutes Chelsea got one back. Then, incredibly Liverpool melted and Chelsea had scored four. Had they exhausted themselves? Just to put the question beyond doubt, Willy Fagan drove in another and Liverpool had a 7-4 victory on their hands.

If the fans now expected to be clobbered with Liverpool wilting in the way they used to in the past after great wins, they were right. Manchester United smacked in five to beat them 5-0 just four days later.

The Reds recovered their form to go 12 games without defeat and found themselves on top of the table. Jack Balmer had an incredible time scoring three hat-tricks in three games in a row. He finished the season as top goalscorer with 28 to his credit in all competitions. Liverpool repeated the pattern of a series of wins followed by defeats to slip down to fifth by February of 1947. They were still battling in the FA Cup and beat Birmingham 4-1 to reach the semi-finals although they lost to Burnley 1-0 in the replay.

The League began to look very hopeful for them as the last matches arrived until the Reds went 7 games without defeat and were once again on top, 2 points clear of Stoke. Liverpool were playing Everton in the Liverpool Senior Cup final when the news came through that Stoke had lost their final game. Liverpool had returned to claim the title.

BILLY LIDDELL SIGNING AUTOGRAPHS 16TH APRIL 1953

And they beat Everton 2-1 for good measure.

Liverpool chairman Billy O'Connell lived long enough to see Liverpool return in triumph. A few months later he was dead. He would have been saddened to know that Liverpool had got to the top of the ladder but were about to slide down the snake in a way no one could have imagined. 15 years would pass before the Kop could once again roar on their champions.

1947/48 did not bring the glory hoped for. Albert Stubbins did not disappoint and hit 24 goals to become top goalscorer for the season but that was not enough. Liverpool came in 11th. The following season the top goalscorer Jack Balmer could manage only 16 goals in all competitions and the Reds dropped another place to 12th.

Billy Liddell became Liverpool's top goalscorer for 7 out of the next 9 years. Yet the goals did not come as easily as they had in the past. Nonetheless, there was an unprecedented run of 19 games without defeat to start the new season, which kicked off with a terrific 4-2 win against Stoke. Liverpool shot to the top of the table. And they began a Cup run which was to take them all the way into the final. There was a wobble when they lost 3-2 to Bolton Wanderers in the new year. Another in February, 4-1 down to Middlesbrough, started a tumble and pointed to the season's end when the last three matches ended in defeat to land the Reds on eighth place. A great disappointment.

But there had been an FA Cup final for only the second time in their history. Liverpool lost 2-0 to Arsenal and Liddell had been physically mistreated by Arsenal but the Liverpool team could be proud of their achievement.

Manager George Kay was taken ill in the off-season and went into hospital. He was unable to train the team again and resigned in January 1951. His loss seemed to derail the team whose season started and ended with defeats and included a 10-game run without a win and 4 defeats. 11th place was all that could be salvaged.

The search for a new manager had passed over the man who would change Liverpool history for ever; Bill was interviewed for the post but did not want the directors interfering in his team selections. Don Welsh from Charlton Athletic was chosen instead.

Ironically the 1952/53 season began well with 4 wins and 3 draws. The team could not sustain this

FA CUP FINAL ARSENAL V LIVERPOOL
JOE MERCER (RIGHT) ARSENAL CAPTAIN
AND LIVERPOOL CAPTAIN, PHIL TAYLOR
29TH APRIL 1950

WEST STANDING ENCLOSURE

ENTER AT TURNSTILES (See Plan on back) H

ENTRANCE 63

EMPIRE STADIUM, WEMBLEY

THE FOOTBALL ASSOCIATION CUP COMPETITION

FINAL TIE

SATURDAY, APRIL 29th, 1950

Kick-off 3 p.m.

Price 3/- (Including Tax)

CHAIRMAN AND MANAGING DIRECTOR, Wembley Stadium Limited

THIS PORTION TO BE RETAINED (See conditions on back)

FA CUP FINAL ARSENAL V LIVERPOOL A GOAL LINE SAVE BY ARSENAL GOALKEEPER GEORGE SWINDIN 29TH APRIL 1950

form and although they were often inspired after a big defeat to come back and win impressively, for example, a 3-0 defeat to West Bromwich brought a 5-3 victory against Newcastle United in its wake, they would more often lose and endured a run of 12 games without a win. Chelsea and Liverpool had to battle to stay in the Division and Liverpool pulled it off with a 2-0 win. The Reds were down on 17th place.

Starting the new season of 1953/54 with a victory seemed a bad omen, oddly, and so it proved to be. Two draws against Manchester United and Newcastle United seemed to foretell of better things to come. Instead there were 5 defeats in as many games. It was symbolic that full back Eddie Spicer suffered a terrible leg injury in December when he received a kick that shattered his leg. His career was ruined.

4 victories in April could not stop Liverpool from taking up last position and being relegated to Division Two for the first time in 50 years. It was a bitter experience. Lacking proper support, Liddell's talents had been wasted. Without him, as one newspaper pointed out, it was horrible to contemplate where the Reds might have been.

Manager George Kay who had lived for the club, also died in April. Life at Liverpool was indeed going to be different next season.

The climb out of the Second Division took longer than anyone thought it might. There was to be no immediate promotion this time. Don Welsh remained in his job and Liddell became captain again becoming top goalscorer in all competitions in the 1954/55 season. The results were mixed, wins following defeats and draws with Liverpool suffering their worst ever defeat

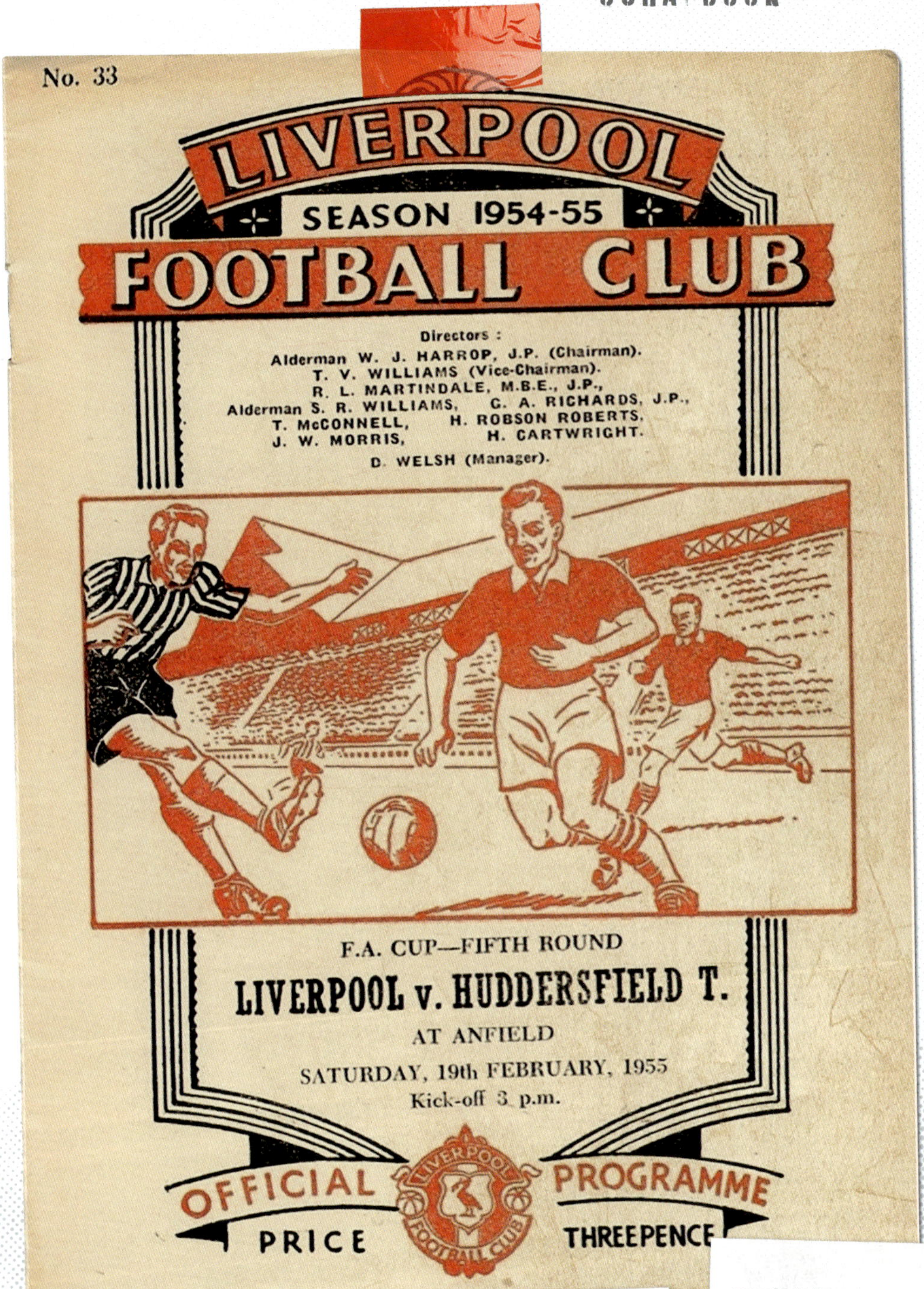

LIVERPOOL'S SECOND GOAL SCORED AGAINST MALMO AT RASUNDA STADIUM 20TH MAY 1951

in December against Birmingham losing 9-1. They then lost 4-1 to Doncaster Rovers before hammering 6 past Ipswich Town in a 6-2 victory. There was a glorious 4-0 win against Everton in the FA Cup 4th round but Huddersfield knocked them out of the Cup in the 5th, 2-0. An indifferent season found them on 11th place as it ended.

Welsh knew his job was now at stake But part of his problem was interference by the Liverpool Board of Directors who were entitled to select the teams. Their lack of ability in this area was having predictable results.

Billy Liddell was again on fine form in the 1955/56 season scoring 32 goals in all competitions and this time his efforts brought Liverpool to 3rd place in the table. It is a credit to him that he did not ask to be transferred so that he could play in the First Division, which is where his talents belonged. On the 23rd November 1957 Liddell would break the record for appearances at Liverpool in his 469th game, when he scored two goals in the 2-0 win against Blackburn.

Welsh, however, was not to be given another chance and he was dismissed. In his place came Phil Taylor

a former Liverpool captain who was on the coaching staff. Taylor brought in a whole raft of new players such as Tommy Younger as goalkeeper, Jimmy Harrower an attacking midfielder from Hibernian and Johnny Wheeler from Bolton Wanderers. And there were younger players also coming through such as Ronnie Moran and Jimmy Melia. These changes enabled a corner to be turned and the slide down the table to ignominy could be stopped.

At the end of the 1956/57 season Liverpool had fought their way back into 3rd place again. There had been two good spells that had brought 4 wins in 4 matches each, and 4 wins in the last 5 matches gave the supporters heart.

The following season they were in fourth place. The Reds were managing to hold their own despite worrying slip-ups like a 6-1 defeat against Cardiff City. But when they reached 4th place again in the 1958/59 season the alarm bells were beginning to ring. Were Liverpool no longer capable of First Division football?

Four losses in the first eight matches of the 1959/60 season seemed to answer the question.

" . . . Phil Tayor resigned on the 17th November . . ." was part of a statement by the club that showed the anxiety in the boardroom. It was an historic statement, too, for without anyone realising, it had announced the beginning of a new era at Liverpool that would slowly usher in years of glory that could only be dreamed of until then.

A man had been appointed manager who would become one of the elite managers whose names are legendary throughout the football world.

## THE MAN WAS BILL SHANKLY.

# THE GLORIOUS 1960s

In December 1960 Shankly saw his team win three and lose two matches. He had taken charge on the 19th December and the team rewarded him with 2 defeats, 0-4 against Cardiff city and 0-3 against Charlton Athletic. But there were only 4 more defeats and the Reds played 7 successive games without defeat to end the season.

Billy Liddell was brought back into the side for ten games and although he was 38 years old, his presence made all the difference. Young Roger Hunt had proven his worth by scoring 23 goals in all competitions. Liverpool edged back up into third place. At least Shankly had stopped the team from sliding. But he knew he needed to do more if Liverpool were to be worthy of a First Division place and in the off-season he was out scouting for talent. Alf Arrowsmith, Tommy Smith, Gordon Wallace and Bobby Graham were four of the boys who caught Shankly's eye.

The first eight games of the 1960/61 season disappointed Shankly as 4 of them were lost. This was not the stuff of champions. *"Deplorable"* was his word for the performances and he decided that a radical change was needed. He set his hopes on a 3-3-4 formation in which Jimmy Harrower was moved from inside left to be used as a semi-halfback. The idea was that the opposing halfback would be drawn from his position and Harrower could feed his two wingers for their attacks. A glorious run of 14 games without loss helped to maintain the Reds' position in the League but they lost momentum again and at the end of Shankly's first full season in charge the team was back in the familiar third place.

Shankly was suffering as his predecessors had done from lack of understanding amongst the members of the Liverpool Board. He knew that he needed to buy top-class players to enable Liverpool to step into the First Division. The Board, however, did not allow him to do this. Their attitude might have doomed Liverpool. So it was an incredible stroke of luck for Shankly and Liverpool that Eric Sawyer, an accountant with Littlewoods Pools, was nominated to take a place on the Board. He was in tune with Shankly's thinking and from then on the Shankly was free to go and find, and more importantly, sign the top-quality players he needed.

One of Shankly's first top-quality players to sign for Liverpool was the Scot Ian St. John of Motherwell and it was to Scotland that Shankly turned to bolster the Liverpool defence.

This time the man was Ronnie Yeats a 23-year-old playing for Dundee United. Shankly put together a winning team and from the very first whistle of the 1961/62 season they were out to prove that they were a team ready to challenge for the top place. They notched up 6 wins before their first draw, which they then followed up with another 4 victories. Only Middlesbrough brought their undefeated run to an end. The next match brought back memories of the past as they slammed 6 past Walsall and then crumpled 0-2 to Derby County. Significantly, there had been a feast of goals already with five pushed in against Leeds and Bury and another five waiting to hit Swansea City, Norwich City and in revenge, Middlesbrough. Roger Hunt made sure they kept coming by scoring 42 in all competitions with 5 hat-tricks. He was often fed balls by a tireless Ian St. John. Yeats had been at Anfield for just five months when he was made captain on the 26th December 1961. He did not relinquish his grip on the captaincy for ten

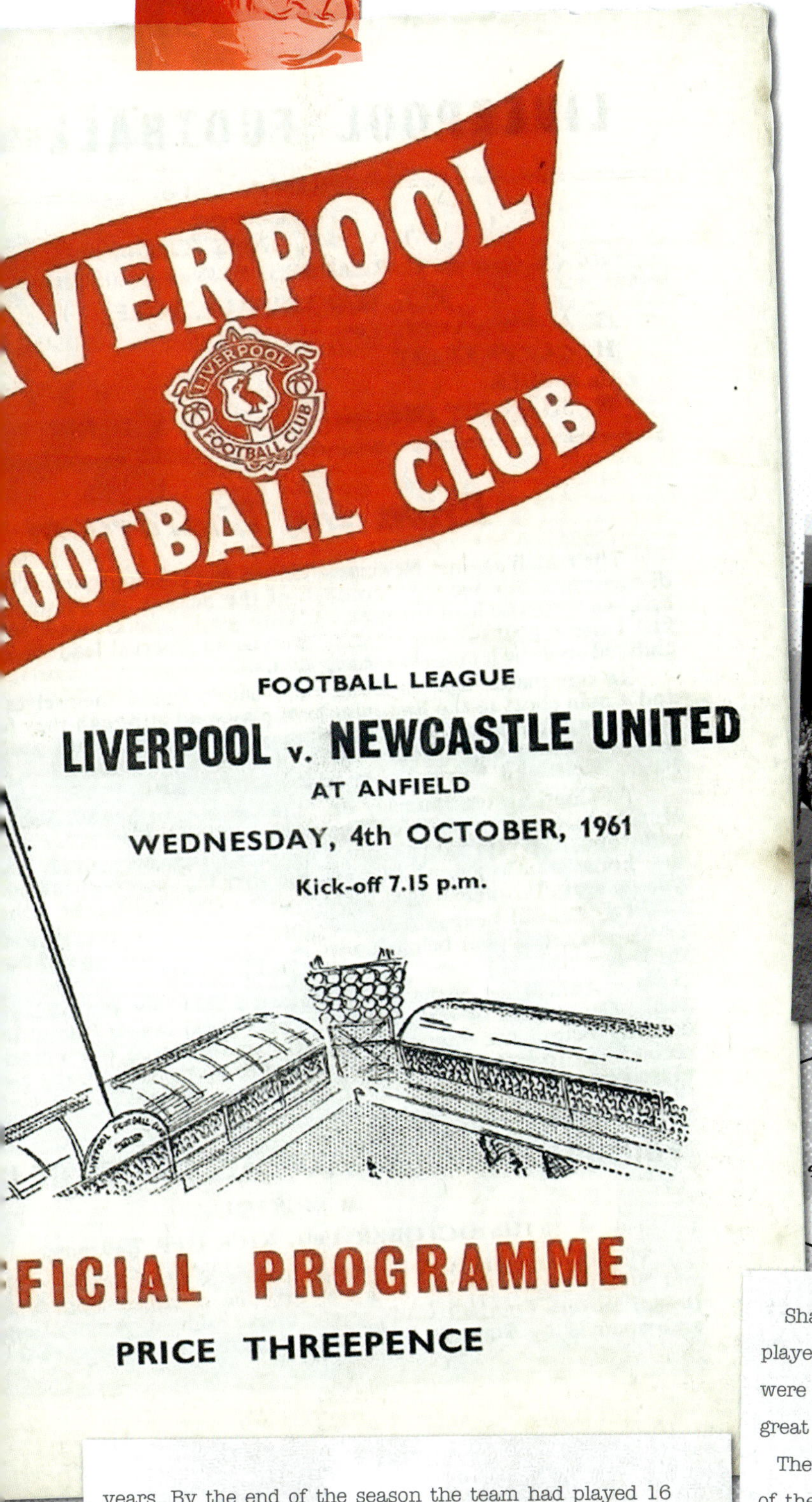


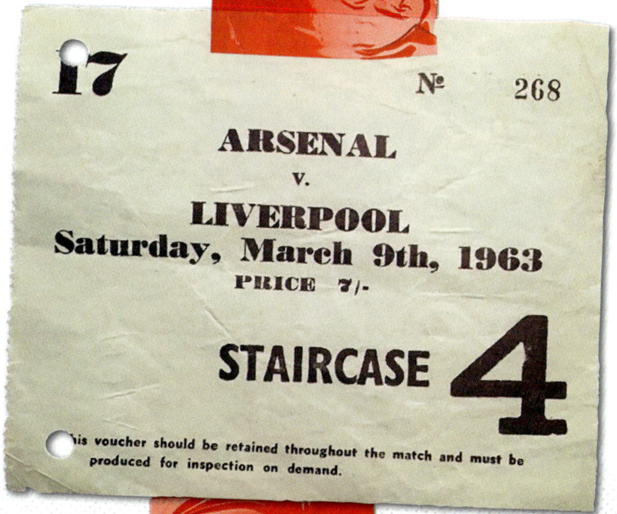

LIVERPOOL MAKE A LAP OF HONOUR BEFORE THE CHEERING ANFIELD CROWD AFTER THE 5-0 VICTORY OVER ARSENAL WHICH GAVE THEM THE LEAGUE CHAMPIONSHIP 20TH APRIL 1964

years. By the end of the season the team had played 16 games in which they had not conceded a single goal.

By the 21st April 1962 and the match against Southampton at Anfield Liverpool had played so well that they needed just one point to get back into the First Division. Liverpool were flying high and they came away 2-0 winners. Eight years of penance had been put to an end; the Reds were set to return to Division One.

Shankly had improved the fitness levels of the Liverpool players and shown that with improved tactics, his men were capable of great things. And Shankly wanted those great things. Promotion was just the beginning.

There were five losses in twelve matches at the beginning of the 1962/63 season. It was not the best start and Liverpool were soon down near the relegation zone.

In September Liverpool lined up for a very special game. Their opponents were Everton and the two teams had not met competitively since January 1955. It was a dramatic match with Hunt coming to the rescue for Liverpool just before the final whistle so that the Reds came away with a 2-2 draw.

Shankly knew there were weak points in the team and

SPURS V LIVERPOOL, ROGER HUNT SCORES DESPITE THE EFFORTS OF SPURS GOALKEEPER HOLLOWBREAD & RIGHT BACK RON HENRY 27TH MARCH 1964

he bought Willie Stevenson for midfield. Stevenson was an excellent reader of the game and he was joined on the team by Tommy Lawrence, a 22-year-old Liverpool boy. Lawrence had signed for Liverpool at the age of 17. Now his chance had come, he would not be dislodged from his position for another 7 years.

Liverpool hauled themselves back up to the middle of the table and also had a good run in the FA Cup only losing out to Leicester City in the semi-final 1-0. But the final polish that would make a serious challenge for the title viable, was still missing, as four games that season would prove. Liverpool beat Tottenham Hotspur 5-2 and Manchester United 1-0 only to then lose immediately against Tottenham Hotspur 7-2 and Nottingham Forest 2-0 at Anfield. Nonetheless the Reds managed to finish the season in eighth place. Shankly made just one signing during the summer of 1964. It was an inspired one. He signed Peter Thompson a brilliant right-footed left winger who could turn his opponents into knots.

Stretching their supporters' nerves to breaking point, Liverpool managed to lose 2 of their first 3 games in the 1963/64 season. There were two away wins before a third defeat at home to West Ham United 1-2. Shankly, so the story goes, marched into a directors' board meeting to announce *"I can assure you, gentlemen, that we will win a game at Anfield this season."* He then turned on his heel and stalked out of the room.

Shankly was apparently as forceful with his players as he was with the board because in the very next game against Wolves the Reds whacked in 6 goals in a 6-0 victory. Perhaps, just for the sake of tradition, after a mighty victory they lost 3-0 to Sheffield United.

But in amongst the defeats, which were becoming rare events, there was blistering attacking football; 6-1 against Stoke City, 5-0 against Derby, 6-1 against Sheffield United, 6-0 against Ipswich Town. And by November Liverpool had reached the heady heights to sit on top of the First Division. Hunt was having the time of his life and hit home 31 League goals that season.

From the middle of March the Reds hit their stride winning seven games in a row, in one of which they hammered three past a Manchester United team boasting the talents of Best, Charlton and Law. And there was one final glorious victory still to come. If Liverpool could win against Arsenal on the 18th April they would be First Division champions.

Thanks to an incredible penalty save by keeper Lawrence Liverpool ran off the pitch at half-time 2-0 in the lead. And in the second half it got better. In the fifty-second minute Thompson, who was having a brilliant game, slammed in the third goal and followed it up 5 minutes later with the fourth. Not to be outdone Roger Hunt let loose with a long-range shot to score Liverpool's fifth. The Reds had done it. The championship title was theirs.

Shanks, as he was now known, could not pull off the same trick the following season, however. Instead he guided the team towards different honours.

The league started badly with 2 defeats in 3 games, which were followed shortly by 3 further defeats against

LIVERPOOL PLAYERS CELEBRATE IN THEIR DRESSING ROOM AT ANFIELD AFTER CLINCHING THE LEAGUE CHAMPIONSHIP 18TH APRIL 1964

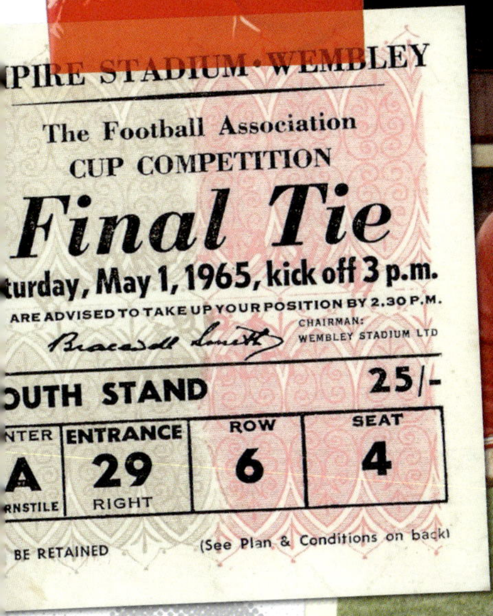
IPIRE STADIUM · WEMBLEY
The Football Association
CUP COMPETITION
Final Tie
turday, May 1, 1965, kick off 3 p.m.
ARE ADVISED TO TAKE UP YOUR POSITION BY 2.30 P.M.
CHAIRMAN: WEMBLEY STADIUM LTD
OUTH STAND 25/-

| NTER | ENTRANCE | ROW | SEAT |
|---|---|---|---|
| A | 29 | 6 | 4 |
| RNSTILE | RIGHT | | |

BE RETAINED (See Plan & Conditions on back)

THE BOOT ROOM BOYS (L-R) BILL SHANKLY, BOB PAISLEY, RONNIE MORAN, JOE FAGAN AND REUBEN BENNETT, 1960'S AT ANFIELD

Leicester City, Sheffield Wednesday and Everton. This stumble proved to be too much for them to overcome and they finished in 7th place.

In their first European Cup match against Icelandic team Knattspyrnufélag Reykjavíkur, Liverpool came away 5-0 winners beating them again 6-1 in the second leg. Liverpool went through to the semi-final against Milan beating the Italians 3-1 at home but losing 3-0 in Italy. Apparently, Shankly had been told before the game that Liverpool would not go through to the final and the referee saw to it that two goals by Milan that violated the rules were allowed.

By then, however, there had been a magnificent FA Cup run that brought Liverpool to a semi-final against League leaders Chelsea.

Considering that they had played Cologne in the European Cup in midweek the Reds' 2-0 win was

THE FA CUP FINAL AT WEMBLEY LIVERPOOL 2 LEEDS UNITED 1. THE FAMED LEEDS DEFENSIVE SYSTEM IN ACTION IN THE MATCH 1ST MAY 1965

remarkable. And it put Liverpool into the FA Cup final bringing every Liverpudlian's dream one step closer.

On the 1st May 1965 Liverpool ran out onto the Wembley pitch against Leeds United to make history. For most of the match neither side could take control. Hunt broke the stalemate in the 93rd minute only to see Leeds equalise 7 min later. For the first time since 1947 the FA Cup final went into extra time.

Liverpool's left-back Byrne had been playing with a broken collarbone for most of the match. But he got his reward for his courage when Ian St. John scored the winning goal in the 111th minute. Liverpool had won the FA Cup.

It was a day when grown men cried and one of the greatest moments in the history of Liverpool Football Club. Shanks had kept his word.

THE FA CUP FINAL AT WEMBLEY STADIUM LIVERPOOL CAPTAIN, RON YEATS SMILES AS HE IS CONGRATULATED BY THE QUEEN AFTER RECEIVING THE TROPHY 1ST MAY 1965

1966 EUROPEAN CUP WINNERS CUP SEMI FINAL CELTIC V LIVERPOOL CELTIC CAPTAIN BILLY MCNEILL EXCHANGES PENNANTS WITH RON YEATS 14TH APRIL 1966

LIVERPOOL FOOTBALL CLUB
FOOTBALL LEAGUE DIVISION 1
LIVERPOOL v. LEEDS UTD.
AT ANFIELD
Saturday, Nov. 19th, 1966
Kick-off 3-00 p.m.
Main Stand Block "A"
Entrance Lake Street and Anfield Road
P. B. Robinson
Secretary
THIS PORTION TO BE RETAINED

| ADMISSION | Row | Seat |
|---|---|---|
| 8/- | B | 48 |

Issued subject to the Rules & Regs. of the Football Assn.

The League challenge in the 1965/66th season got off to a sticky start until the Reds got into their stride with a 3-2 win against Blackpool and followed it up with a 5-1 win against West Ham United. Roger Hunt was again lashing in the goals, there would be 33 for him in all competitions this season. In another five-goal feast, Liverpool met Everton again on the 25th September and made hard going of the first half leading by just one goal at half time.

**But when Hunt scored the second goal after the break, Liverpool ran riot to the delight of the fans in the Kop, winning 5-0.**

The FA Cup eluded the team this year with a 2-1 defeat against Chelsea but the European Cup proved to be much more exciting. There was a heart-stopping wait following a 1-0 defeat at Celtic before they won 2-0 in the return match to go through to the final against Borussia Dortmund.

In an untidy, accident-prone match the Reds lost 2-1 but could rightly be proud of having reached the final in only their second outing in the European Cup competition.

There was still a chance of glory in the League,

Liverpool President Tom Williams talks about the club, its success and its future

# WE'VE NEVER HAD A BETTER SET OF LADS

**When I became President of the Liverpool club after many seasons as chairman, I told shareholders at our annual meeting that I thought we had a fine side for at least five seasons to come. What has happened in the past three seasons has more than borne out my confidence in our players and our staff. To win the League championship; then the F.A. Cup; then the championship again in so short a space of time is a fantastic record of achievement and there is no saying where this record of progress will end.**

There is no doubt that Manager Bill Shankly has been the inspiring force behind our success. And not only that, he has also done magnificent work in getting the players fit and keeping them fit. They could not have been better trained.

The fact that we used only 14 players when winning the championship for the second time in three seasons is sufficient indication that our men have been fitter for their tasks. This in itself is a fine tribute to all our training staff, led by Reuben Bennett and Bob Paisley.

They have supervised the training schedules arranged by Mr. Shankly and the players have given them 100 per cent effort on the training ground and on the field. The varied nature of their training makes training less of a chore than it used to be, but one must never forget that footballers can become stale and it is a tribute to our staff and to the players' enthusiasm for their work which has kept our team fresh and vital for their enormous programme over the past few seasons.

## MUCH HARD WORK

They have been put right, tactically, for all their missions. Our success has come after an infinity of hard work. There is no substitute for effort and our players have always made it.

I think our success recently came initially from the League's change of heart over players' rewards. There were times when players would not come to us.

As soon as we were able to pay players what they were worth the position changed. A well-supported club, we were able to go out and get the players we wanted and, moreover, pay them properly. The coming of Ian St. John and Ronnie Yeats was another milestone in our recent history. From that point we started to rise.

It took us long to regain our First Division status, but once we did so the team proved that they were not only good enough to win the First Division title, but also the Cup — and winning the Cup for the first time is probably the greatest triumph we have had in contemporary times.

Our boys are splendid team men. They work together; they do their utmost. Only in this way has the team been able to prove themselves not only as one of the finest sides in Britain, but one of the greatest teams in Europe. I don't think we've ever had a better set of lads. No team could have done more for us.

We've had the support which makes success essential. I don't know better supporters than those to be found on the Kop and I've travelled the world of football. We'll still be a great side next season. The youth, skill is still there. All we want is freedom from injury. Injuries can destroy any team.

I think it is a tribute to the way our boys play that they have suffered so little from physical damage. After so much success we really cannot expect much more, but I don't doubt our side will produce the goods again for us next season. The European Cup, I think, is probably more difficult to win than any other tournament in the world.

## LOOKING FOR TALENT

You've got to be good enough to lick the other side, but you've got to endure strange spectators, fiery opposition and referees who do not always handle the game as well as some of our's do.

**Every club is on the look out for talent, whether they have been succesful or not and we are no exceptions, but the transfer market is a difficult one in more senses than one nowadays. There aren't many clubs who are prepared even to offer any of their good 'uns and when one does they want the earth. We don't want to be bled white.**

**I think the standard of football to-day is higher than ever. The game has changed in many respects. Everything is much more intensified; they've got all the different techniques of play, individual and collective, down to a fine art. Players know what to do when the ball is at their feet and they know what to do when they're without it. It's all very professional and expert and nothing but the best will do.**

**For the smaller clubs in the game, some of whom exist on weekly pools, the future could be bleak, but I wouldn't like to see any of them go out of existince. For us in Liverpool the game could not be more flourishing and I hope it continues to do so and reward the most earnest most enthusiastic, most loyal supporters to found anywhere in the game, in Britain or anywhere in the world.**

28

IT'S

After the Chelsea game, Liverpo... triumphant

# ALL OURS!

Yeats with his make-shift trophy, with Hunt, Stevenson, St. John and Smith, assemble for the round. It's smiles all round (below) in the dressing rooms afterwards.

EUROPEAN CUP WINNERS CUP SEMI FINAL CELTIC V LIVERPOOL RONNIE SIMPSON OF CELTIC CLUTCHES THE BALL FROM LAWLER'S HEAD 14TH APRIL 1966

EUROPEAN CUP WINNERS CUP. BORUSSIA DORTMUND PARADE THE TROPHY AROUND THE PITCH 5TH MAY 1966

EUROPEAN CUP WINNERS' CUP FINAL QUARTER-FINAL AT ANFIELD. LIVERPOOL V HONVED OF BUDAPEST, THE HONVED GOALKEEPER IS HELPLESS AS A LAWLER HEADER ENTERS THE NET 8TH MARCH 1966

however, and by mid-April Liverpool were seven points ahead in the table. They needed just one point to gain the title when they ran out against Chelsea on the 30th of the month. There was still a chance that Leeds could overtake them if the Reds lost their last two games and Leeds won their last five games. When Hunt put in a left-footed shot in the 69th minute for the 2-1 winning goal, Liverpool were safe. Cries of *"We want Shankly!"* echoed around the stadium. The title was Liverpool's again.

Having guided the team to two League titles and an FA Cup, Shankly then altered the make-up of the team, which seemed to cause them to lose their edge.

For the 1967/68 season, Tony Hateley had been brought into the team, a centre-forward known for his heading ability. Now, instead of passing balls through on

1966 EUROPEAN CUP WINNERS CUP SEMI FINAL 2ND LEG CELTIC V LIVERPOOL. IAN ST JOHN CELEBRATES AFTER SMITH HAD SCORED LIVERPOOL'S FIRST GOAL 19TH APRIL 1966

OFFICIAL PROGRAMME 1/-
EUROPEAN CUP WINNERS CUP FINAL TIE
LIVERPOOL
DORTMUND
B.V. BORUSSIA DORTMUND
VERSUS LIVERPOOL
HAMPDEN PARK, GLASGOW.
THURSDAY, 5TH MAY 1966.
KICK-OFF 7.30 P.M.
THE SCOTTISH FOOTBALL ASSOCIATION LIMITED

TOTTENHAM HOTSPUR Football & Athletic Co. Ltd.
№ 2674[illegible]
F.A. CUP, 5th ROUND
Tottenham Hotspur
v
LIVERPOOL
AT WHITE HART LANE
On SATURDAY, 9th MARCH, 1968
Kick-off 2.45 p.m.
5/- GROUND TICKET
The Tottenham Hotspur Company do not Guarantee that the proposed match will be played.
G. W. JONES
Secretary
THIS PORTION TO BE RETAINED
In the event of a postponement this ticket will be valid for the rearranged date.
Thomas Knight & Co. Ltd. The Clock House Press Hoddesdon, Herts

Football Club
LIVERPOOL
v.
MANCHESTER CITY
August 10th, 1968
GROUND TICKET
SPION KOP
This Portion to be Retained
№ 12220

Liverpool Football Club
LIVERPOOL
v.
STOKE CITY
September 20th 1969
MAIN STAND
Block "A"
This Portion to be retained
Row C
Seat 43

IAN CALLAGHAN TAKES ON PHIL BEALE OF TOTTENHAM HOTSPUR DURING A FOOTBALL LEAGUE DIVISION ONE MATCH AT WHITE HART LANE

*Photograph by courtesy of Mercury Press Agency Ltd.*

**LIVERPOOL F.C. 1968-69**

*Back Row, left to right:* **Strong, Clemence, Lawrence, Byrne,**
*Middle Row, left to right:* **R. Paisley, (Trainer), Graham, Hateley, Wall, Ross, Arrowsmith, Thompson,**
*Front Row, left to right:* **R. Bennett (Coach), Callaghan, Hughes, Hunt, Yeats, St. John, Smith, Lawler, W. Shankly (Manager)**

A WHITBREAD GROUP COMPANY

## FIXTURES 1968

FOOTBALL LEAGUE

| 58 | | | F | A |
|---|---|---|---|---|
| g. 10 | Manchester C. | H | | |
| , 14 | Southampton | A | | |
| , 17 | Arsenal | A | | |
| , 20 | Stoke City | H | | |
| , 24 | Sunderland | H | | |
| , 27 | Everton | A | | |
| , 31 | Leeds U. | A | | |
| pt. 4 | League Cup (2) | | | |
| 7 | Queen's Park R. | H | | |
| , 14 | Ipswich T. | A | | |
| , 21 | Leicester C. | H | | |
| , 25 | League Cup (3) | | | |
| , 28 | Wolverhampton W. | A | | |
| t. 5 | Burnley | A | | |
| ,, 8 | Everton | H | | |
| ,, 12 | Manchester U. | H | | |
| ,, 16 | League Cup (4) | | | |
| ,, 19 | Tottenham Hotspur | A | | |
| ,, 26 | Newcastle U. | H | | |
| ,, 30 | League Cup (5) | | | |
| ov. 2 | West Brom. A. | A | | |
| ,, 9 | Chelsea | H | | |
| ,, 16 | Sheffield W. | A | | |
| ,, 20 | League Cup (S.F.) | | | |
| ,, 23 | Coventry C. | H | | |
| ,, 30 | Nottingham F. | A | | |
| ec. 3 | Southampton | H | | |
| ,, 4 | League Cup (S.F.) | | | |
| ,, 7 | West Ham Utd. | H | | |
| ,, 14 | Manchester U. | A | | |
| ,, 21 | Tottenham Hotspur | H | | |
| ,, 26 | Burnley | H | | |
| ,, 28 | Newcastle U. | A | | |

CENTRAL LEAGUE

| 1968 | | | F | A |
|---|---|---|---|---|
| Aug. 10 | Aston Villa | A | | |
| ,, 14 | Leeds U. | H | | |
| ,, 17 | Wolverhampton W. | H | | |
| ,, 21 | Derby County | A | | |
| ,, 24 | Manchester C. | A | | |
| ,, 27 | Sheffield U. | H | | |
| ,, 31 | Bolton W. | H | | |
| Sept. 3 | Stoke C. | H | | |
| ,, 10 | Blackburn R. | H | | |
| ,, 14 | Bury | A | | |
| ,, 24 | Blackpool | H | | |
| ,, 28 | Blackburn R. | A | | |
| Oct. 5 | Sheffield W. | H | | |
| ,, 12 | West Brom A. | A | | |
| ,, 19 | Coventry City | H | | |
| ,, 26 | Preston N.E. | A | | |
| Nov. 2 | Manchester U. | H | | |
| ,, 9 | Everton | A | | |
| ,, 16 | Burnley | H | | |
| ,, 23 | Huddersfield T. | A | | |
| ,, 30 | Nottingham F. | H | | |
| Dec. 7 | Newcastle U. | A | | |
| ,, 14 | West Brom A. | H | | |
| ,, 21 | Coventry City | A | | |
| ,, 26 | Sheffield W. | A | | |
| ,, 28 | Preston N.E. | H | | |

hese Fixtures are the copyright of The Football League Limited, and are printed with their permission nder Licence No. 2. They must not be reproduced in whole or part without permission of The Football League Limited.

Liverpool Litho Limited, Member of the Seel House Press Seel Street, Liverpool 1

the ground, the team was sending them forwards in the air. This had a negative effect on the lads' playing even though Hateley scored 16 League goals that season. Shankly realised his mistake too late although he sold Hateley the following season. Liverpool ended up in fifth position.

Although it seemed a wise move at the time to buy teenager Alun Evans in September 1968 and groom him as a successor to Roger Hunt the teenager failed to live up to expectations. Despite being top of the League over the winter in the 1968/69 season, Liverpool were overtaken by Leeds. They came in second. But a miss is as good as a mile and another year had passed with no trophies. Had Shanks lost his touch?

**THE FANS WOULD HAVE TO ENDURE A FEW YEARS OF DROUGHT BEFORE GLORY CAME THEIR WAY AGAIN.**

JOHN BOYLE OF CHELSEA FC TRACKS EMLYN HUGHES 18TH JANUARY 1968

LIVERPOOL RIGHT HALF TOMMY SMITH (LEFT) ATTEMPTS TO TACKLE WEST HAM'S RON BOYCE AT UPTON PARK 20TH APRIL 1968

# THE 70s & 80s

Shankly's team had burned itself out earlier than he had expected and so he set about rejuvenating the squad. Another Liverpool legend Ray Clemence took up residence between the goalposts and Larry Lloyd came into the defence. John Toshack came to Liverpool from Cardiff and Steve Heighway secured his first League goal, with Liverpool. His ball control was perfect and he could deliver spot-on passes at breathtaking speeds.

The 1970/71 season was the next one to show signs that Liverpool were back on track. They made their way to the FA Cup final against Arsenal only to lose 2-1. And they got as far as the semi-final in the European Fairs Cup only to be defeated by Leeds 1-0. They ended the season in the League in 5th position for the second time in a row.

Shankly now added another man to the team who was to become a jewel in the Liverpool crown. Kevin Keegan.

Despite the new line up, Liverpool did not look like a side heading for a trophy as the 1971/72 season got underway. By November, they were no longer contenders for the European Cup Winners' Cup or the League Cup. Life in the League was proving difficult, too, with six defeats in the first twelve matches. By the New Year they were still only in ninth place. The FA Cup disappeared from view in February with a 2-0 defeat to Leeds. And then, as so often in the past, the defeat seemed to inspire them and they powered through thirteen games without defeat hammering three past Manchester City four past Everton and five past Newcastle United. With two games to play, they

KEVIN KEEGAN 1972

JOHN TOSHACK BEATS EVERTON'S HENRY NEWTON IN THE AIR 10TH APRIL 1972

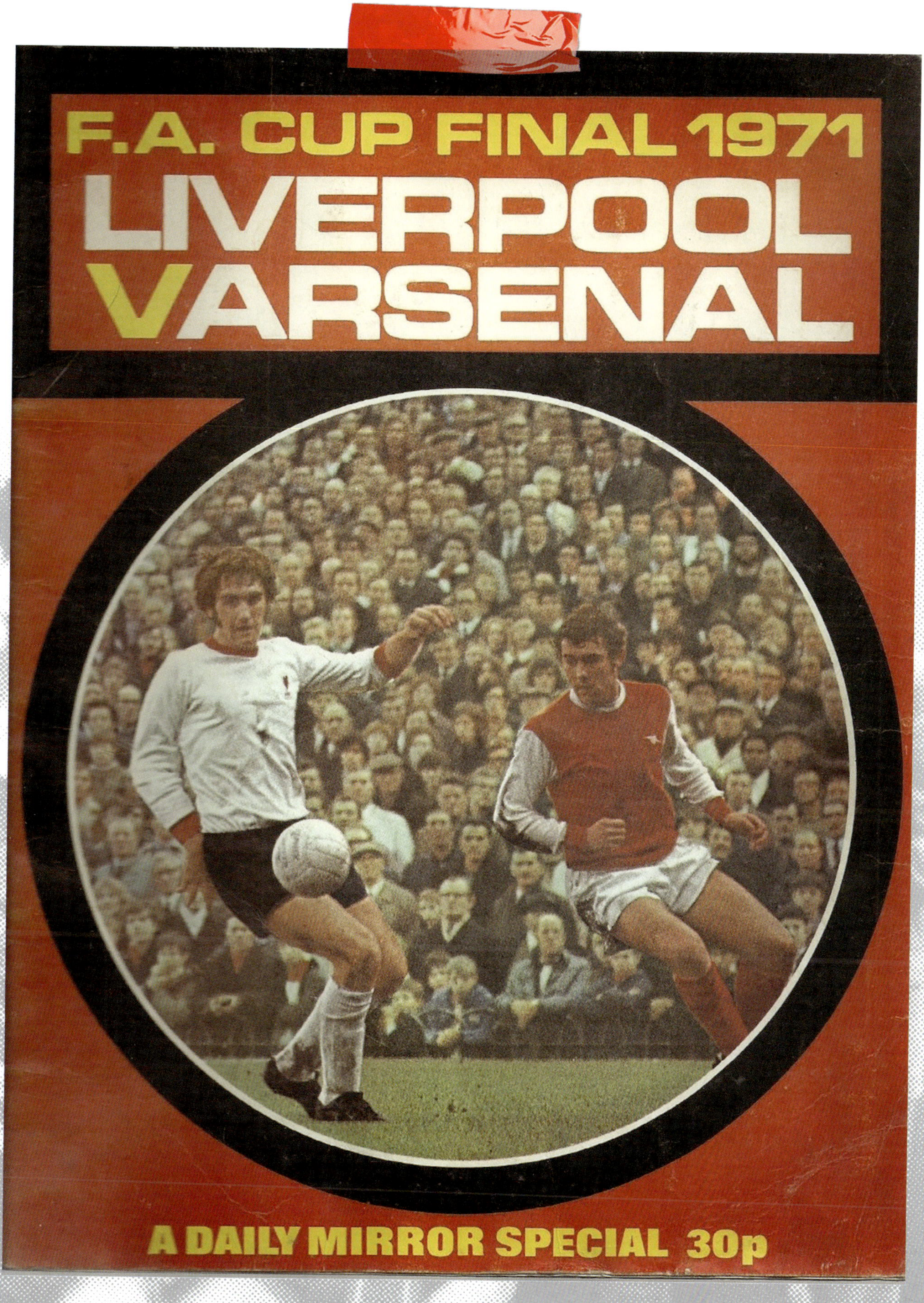
F.A. CUP FINAL 1971
LIVERPOOL
V ARSENAL
A DAILY MIRROR SPECIAL 30p

were back in contention for the title alongside Derby, Leeds and Manchester City. Liverpool faltered losing 1-0 to Derby and drawing 0-0 with Arsenal in the last game of the season. Just one point separated them from Derby who took the league title. Liverpool were in third place. A disappointing season then, but one that had proven that Liverpool could stay the course and that Shanks had put together a top-class team. The drought was over and the glorious years were about to begin.

Four wins and a draw got the Reds off to a good start in the 1972/73 season. Ian Callaghan played his 535th game for the club beating Billy Liddell's record number of appearances. Two defeats were followed by an eighteen-game run without defeat, which included matches when they put five past Carlisle United and Sheffield United and beat rival Manchester City 1-0. Even the loss of John Toshack who had been injured in the middle of September - by which time he had scored six goals in seven games - could not stop the onslaught. Toshack, by the way, had scored seventeen goals by the end of the season in all competitions, second only to Kevin Keegan.

By February of 1973 Tottenham Hotspur had a stop put to Liverpool's run in the League Cup with a 3-1 defeat and Manchester City had put paid to their FA Cup hopes with a 2-0 defeat in a replay. But the Reds were having a good run in the UEFA Cup and by the end of March they had disposed of Dynamo Dresden, winning 2-0 at Anfield and 1-0 in Germany. They met Tottenham Hotspur in the semi-final and revenge was indeed sweet. Liverpool won at Anfield 1-0.

Before the replay took place, the Reds were sitting at the top of the League table and Shankly was confident enough to announce *"I think we can call ourselves champions now."* Liverpool would have to lose their last game and Arsenal win their last to draw level but Liverpool had a better goal average.

Liverpool were made to fight to the last minute at the replay at White Hart Lane against Tottenham. Tottenham scored a goal and the teams were level pegging. Steve Heighway put Liverpool back in contention but when Martin Peters levelled the aggregate scores with another goal, the last 15 min of the match kept the Liverpool supporters on tenterhooks. But when the final whistle went,

UEFA CUP FINAL SECOND LEG MATCH IN MUNICH. BORUSSIA MUNCHENGLADBACH 2 V LIVERPOOL 0. CELEBRATIONS FOR LIVERPOOL AS THEY WIN THEIR FIRST EUROPEAN TROPHY WITH KEVIN KEEGAN CARRIED ON FANS SHOULDERS AFTER THEY INVADED THE PITCH, 23RD MAY 1973

Liverpool had won thanks to that crucial Heighway away goal. Liverpool were into the final.

**Just 3 days later Liverpool met Leicester City in the League. The 0-0 draw was enough to secure them the League title.**

Liverpool's opponents in the UEFA Cup final were the German team Borussia Mönchengladbach, which boasted a raft of gifted players. This time luck was on Shankly's side because he made the decision to have his team play a passing game. John Toshack was dropped in favour of Brian Hall. This decision could have proved fatal if monsoon conditions had not forced the referee to abandon the game when it was barely half an hour old. During that half an hour however, Shankly had realised that the Germans were having problems with high crosses in their penalty area.

When the game was replayed Toshack was back at the front, Shankly had recognised his mistake. Toshack ran riot in the German half and set up both of Kevin Keegan's goals. Had Keegan not missed a penalty, the final score line would have been even more impressive. There was a third goal headed in by Larry Lloyd and an outstanding save by Ray Clemence that like Heighway's goal against Tottenham, proved to be vital.

The Germans were not so easy to push over in the second leg and swirled around Liverpool,

LIVERPOOL FIRST TEAM SQUAD 1ST JULY 1974

netting two before half time. Suddenly, the Reds were in danger of letting the cup slip from their grasp. On aggregate Liverpool was still one goal ahead; the second half was going to be a tense affair for Liverpool fans. Fortunately, the Germans seemed to have exhausted themselves in the first half and with tenacious defending, Liverpool managed to keep them away from the goal. When the whistle blew, Liverpool had won the UEFA Cup, and the League Cup was theirs, too.

The team was absolutely shattered. *"The happiest day of my life" said Shankly. "I wanted that title more than at any time in my life."*

Shankly considered this to be the best team he had ever had. His system had paid handsome dividends. If his players proved that they were worthy of a first-team place then he would keep them there despite a heavy schedule of games. But equally he was careful of their workload on the pitch. *"We didn't want players running the length of the field . . . So our back men played in one area and passed onto the midfield men in their area and so on to the front men."*

## What might this team do the 1973/74 season?

The answer was they would lose just one game in twenty-one in the League yet lose out to Leeds United. Red Star Belgrade put them out of the European Cup but they powered through the FA Cup to reach the final.

Liverpool ran out to meet Newcastle United on 4 May 1974 in what turned out to be one of the most one-sided FA Cup finals ever. Liverpool were unstoppable and Kevin Keegan scored twice and Steve Heighway once. Liverpool had another cup to celebrate.

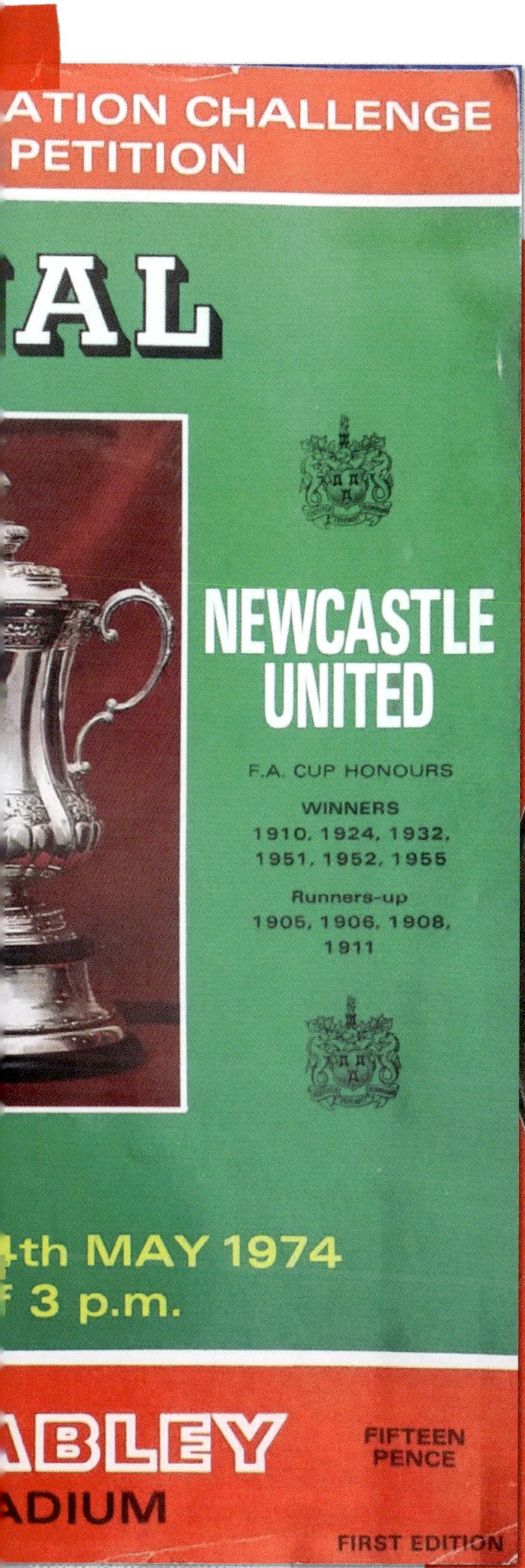
ATION CHALLENGE
PETITION
AL
NEWCASTLE
UNITED
F.A. CUP HONOURS
WINNERS
1910, 1924, 1932, 1951, 1952, 1955
Runners-up
1905, 1906, 1908, 1911
4th MAY 1974
f 3 p.m.
BLEY
ADIUM
FIFTEEN PENCE
FIRST EDITION

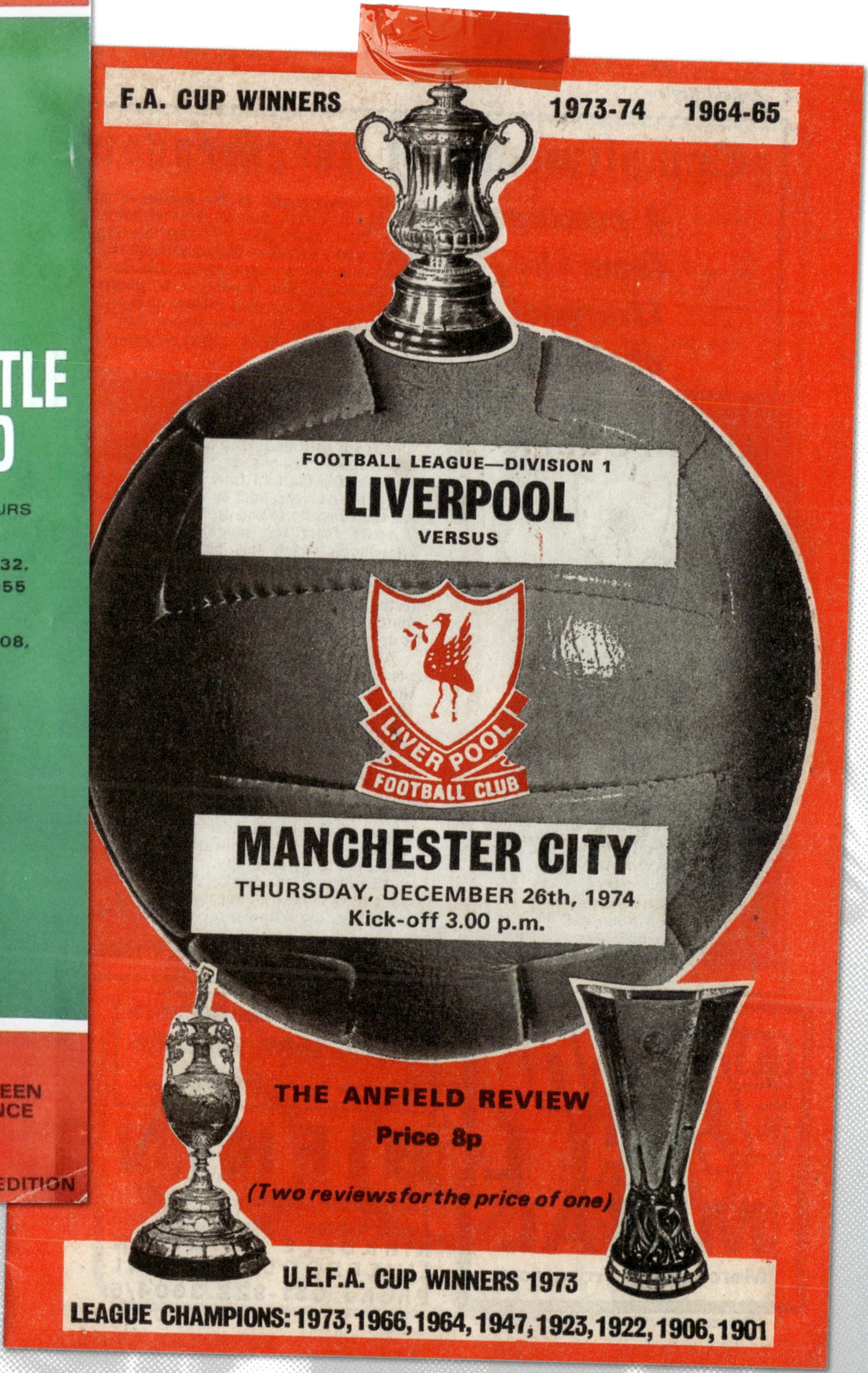
F.A. CUP WINNERS 1973-74 1964-65
FOOTBALL LEAGUE—DIVISION 1
LIVERPOOL
VERSUS
LIVERPOOL FOOTBALL CLUB
MANCHESTER CITY
THURSDAY, DECEMBER 26th, 1974
Kick-off 3.00 p.m.
THE ANFIELD REVIEW
Price 8p
(Two reviews for the price of one)
U.E.F.A. CUP WINNERS 1973
LEAGUE CHAMPIONS: 1973, 1966, 1964, 1947, 1923, 1922, 1906, 1901

# THANKS SHANKS, ALL THE VERY BEST!

LIVERPOOL ECHO HEADLINE

JOHN TOSHACK

### And then the bomb exploded.

At the age of 61 Bill Shankly chose to resign as manager. *"All the arguments had been won"* as he put it himself. *After the FA Cup win Shankly said "I was satisfied and I was tired."* The shockwaves were felt throughout Liverpool.

On the 26th July 1974 Shankly's right-hand man for fifteen years, Bob Paisley, was named as the new manager. He did not take the step lightly and had to be persuaded before he did. According to his wife, one of his reasons for accepting what looked like a poisoned chalice was that he did not want a new man to change what Shankly had begun. Stepping into Shankly shoes was, as Paisley described it, *". . . like being given the Queen Elizabeth to steer in a force 10 gale."*

Paisley's first season as manager started well enough even though Kevin Keegan was sent off in the first match, the Charity Shield at Wembley, which Liverpool won 6-5 on penalties. The only trophy that they would garner that season. They only lost one game out of the first ten, before losing twice to Burnley and then Sheffield United both 1-0.

One of those 10 games was a European Cup Winners' Cup match against the Norwegian side Strømsgodset, which brought the Reds their biggest-ever victory in club history; 11-0. As the team stumbled and then were knocked out of the European competition they stumbled in the League again losing to Ipswich Town and Arsenal. Immediately after that, Middlesbrough put them out of the League Cup 1-0. When they met Ipswich Town again in the FA Cup 4th round they were defeated yet again 1-0. They eventually ended second in the league table just one point behind the leaders Derby. Liverpool was still a

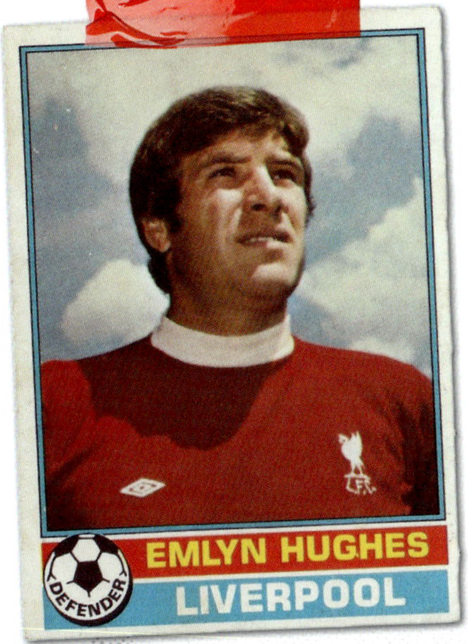

side to reckon with.

Paisley bought in Phil Neal before the next season, which worked wonders with Ray Kennedy's game and earned Neal a permanent place in the team that gelled so well it was soon heading for another double. They slipped up to Burnley in the League Cup but were in top form in the UEFA Cup when they scored a blistering 6-0 win against Real Sociedad in the second round.

The form continued in the League, too, with an eight-game run without defeat. Queens Park Rangers were one point ahead of Liverpool as the season drew to a close but Liverpool had one game left to play against Wolves. This time they did not let the championship slip. They needed just a draw to win on goal average. They kept the fans guessing until the second half when the floodgates certainly opened with Keegan, Toshack and Ray Kennedy flashed in three for the Reds. 3-1 was a fitting end to a championship-winning season. And there was still more excitement to come. Liverpool had reached the UEFA Cup final.

With a 3-2 win at Anfield Liverpool set out for Belgium with high hopes. There was a heart-stopping moment when a penalty put Bruges ahead but Kevin Keegan had soon scored the equaliser and cup-winning goal. Liverpool had won the League and UEFA Cup double twice in four seasons. A remarkable record. And there were more delights in store for the fans the following season 1976/77.

Kevin Keegan's announcement that he was going to

CHARLIE GEORGE DERBY COUNTY GETS TO GRIPS WITH LIVERPOOL'S KEVIN KEEGAN AT THE BASEBALL GROUND LEAGUE DIVISION ONE 28TH FEB 1976

DAVID FAIRCLOUGH POWERS AWAY

PETER EASTOE (QPR) TAKES ON EMLYN HUGHES 7TH MAY 1977

leave the club was a great shock. His decision to stay on for a year and try to get the European Cup with the club proved to be the best of his career.

Liverpool started the League with three wins in three games and at the end of the season they once again sat aloft at the top of the division. There was also a magnificent FA Cup run which produced a delightful 3-0 defeat of Everton but which ended at Wembley in the final with a 2-0 defeat to Manchester United.

The club's European Cup run received a severe blow against St Etienne when they lost 1-0. The return match went down in Liverpool history as a nail-biter. Kevin Keegan put Liverpool into the lead only to see the French side draw level with a spectacular swerving strike from Dominique Bathenay. Even though Ray Kennedy was able to put in a second for Liverpool, the Reds would still lose on the away goals rule unless they could score one more. The minutes ticked away. Toshack was tiring when Paisley made one of the best decisions of his career. He put on the young David Fairclough to replace Toshack. When the youngster got hold of the ball, there were just six minutes left to play. He took the ball forward leaving the defender behind him and the ball was in the net. Liverpool were through to the final.

The Reds were already League champions when they met Borussia Mönchengladbach again in the European Cup final. It was a magnificent match for Liverpool, and Kevin Keegan played the best football he had ever played for the team.

Liverpool were one up at half-time, Tommy Smith put them two up with his first goal for two and a half years and a penalty gave Liverpool their third, and their European Cup dream came true. Bob Paisley did not touch a drop of alcohol that night and the stories surrounding the reasons for his abstinence are many. One of them concerns the lack of Guinness in Rome! A magnificent year came to an end.

LIVERPOOL FOOT[...]

SEMI-FINAL

THE FOOTBALL LEAGUE CUP

SOUVENIR

● GOAL! And Arsenal defender David O'Leary sees the ball whizzing past him for Liverpool's second goal in our 2-0 win the last time the Gunners played here. That was last April, as Liverpool powered their way to the title.

THE ANFIELD REVIEW PRICE 20p

FOOTBALL LEAGUE CUP
Semi-final (First leg)

Tuesday, 7th February, 1978

Kick-off 7.30 p.m.

LIVERPOOL
versus
ARSENAL

WHAT'S INSIDE

- The League Cup—facts and figures about the semi-finalists, and all the previous finals
- The European Cup—spotlight on Benfica, the Eagles of Lisbon
- Arsenal under the microscope, in stories and pictures

Liverpool Football Club

LIVERPOOL F C
v.
F C ZURICH
(SWITZERLAND)

20th APRIL, 1977

GROUND TICKET
SPION KOP

Nº 888

This Portion to be retained.

# CHAMPIONS

THE EMPIRE STADIUM, WEMBLEY

No ticket genuine unless it carries a Lion's Head watermark below

EUROPEAN CHAMPION CLUBS' CUP COMPETITION

**FINAL TIE**

**WED., MAY 10, 1978**

KICK-OFF 7.15 p.m.

YOU ARE ADVISED TO TAKE UP YOUR POSITION BY 6.45 p.m.

TURNSTILES **E**

ENTRANCE **85**

ROW **19**

SEAT **24**

J. S. [signature] CHAIRMAN: WEMBLEY STADIUM LTD

NORTH STAND SEAT
£8.00

TO BE RETAINED

SEE PLAN AND CONDITIONS ON BACK

# OF EUROPE!

ALAN HANSEN, KENNY DALGLISH AND GRAEME SOUNESS CELEBRATE WITH THE CUP 10TH MAY 1978

Keegan kept his word and left for Hamburg before the 1977/78 season. In the search for a replacement, Paisley struck gold. Bill Shankly could not understand how Celtic could let go of such a brilliant player as Kenny Dalglish but they did. And he was top Liverpool goalscorer that season with 31 goals in all competitions. He scored in his first two matches, saving Liverpool's blushes against Middlesbrough in 1-1 draw and helping them in a 2-0 win against Newcastle. In fact the Reds got off to a roaring start with only one defeat in 16 matches. Their European Cup season also got off to a sparkling start at Anfield when they walloped five past Dynamo Dresden in a 5-1 victory.

In January another Liverpool legend joined the team; Graeme Souness. His goal against Manchester United won the BBC goal of the season award. He had one of the most powerful boots in football. Unfortunately, three defeats in five games in January wrecked their chances of another title in the League.

But they were about to set up another record. After the 3-2 defeat by Birmingham City that month, Liverpool would play another 85 games at home without being defeated.

Liverpool thundered forward in the European Cup and European Super Cup games. Hamburg SV were torn to pieces 6-0 in the European Super Cup perhaps leaving Kevin Keegan wishing he had never left Liverpool. But there was another one of those anxious waits when Liverpool met their old rivals Borussia Mönchengladbach in the first leg of the European semi-final and left themselves with a 2-1 deficit to make good. The fans need not have worried with Dalglish helping Liverpool to a 3-0 win at Anfield to take them to a Wembley final against their other old rivals, Bruges. In the 65th minute, the two new boys Kenny Dalglish and Graeme Souness conspired in the

FOOTBALL LEAGUE CUP FINAL
Saturday 18 March 1978 · 3pm
LIVERPOOL V NOTTINGHAM FOREST
Wembley
Stadium
Official Souvenir Programme 30p

THE EMPIRE STADIUM, WEMBLEY
EUROPEAN CHAMPION CLUBS' CUP COMPETITION
No ticket genuine unless it carries a Lion's Head watermark below
FINAL TIE
WED., MAY 10, 1978
TURNSTILES G ENTRANCE 51
KICK-OFF 7.15 p.m.
YOU ARE ADVISED TO TAKE UP YOUR POSITION BY 6.45 p.m.
CHAIRMAN: WEMBLEY STADIUM LTD
682
WEST LOWER STANDING ENCLOSURE
STANDING £2.50
TO BE RETAINED
SEE PLAN AND CONDITIONS ON BACK

STEVE HEIGHWAY 1978

Dalglish goal that took the European Cup to Liverpool. Dalglish had cleverly noted the Belgian goalkeeper's habits and tapped the ball in over his head. Paisley had proved that he was more than just a worthy successor to the great Bill Shankly. He was a great manager in his own right.

The next season 1978/79 proved the reverse of the season before. Kenny Dalglish was rampant in front of the goal scoring an incredible 54 goals in all competitions. The team won ten of their first eleven games before falling foul of rivals Everton in a 1-0 defeat. But there was a 7-0 thrashing of Tottenham to relish, still remembered as one of the greatest games in the history of the club. The last goal was a cracker. Ray Kennedy picked up the ball from Clemence and gave it on to Dalglish who sent it on to Johnson who found Heighway. He hit the ball on the run and as it sailed over to the Tottenham goal McDermott, who had almost run the entire length of the pitch, hit the ball with a power-driven header to score Liverpool's last goal. Kenny Dalglish was made captain of the team halfway through the season before the captaincy passed to Phil Thompson.

Liverpool remained top of the league for 41 games starting the home run in fine style by beating Bolton Wanderers 4-0 and ending the same way by beating Leeds United 3-0. For many, the team that season was the best team Liverpool ever fielded. With men such as Ray Kennedy, Graeme Souness, Kenny Dalglish and David Johnson in the team, they may well have been right. They all helped to create a Football League record when the team gained 68 points conceding just 16 goals.

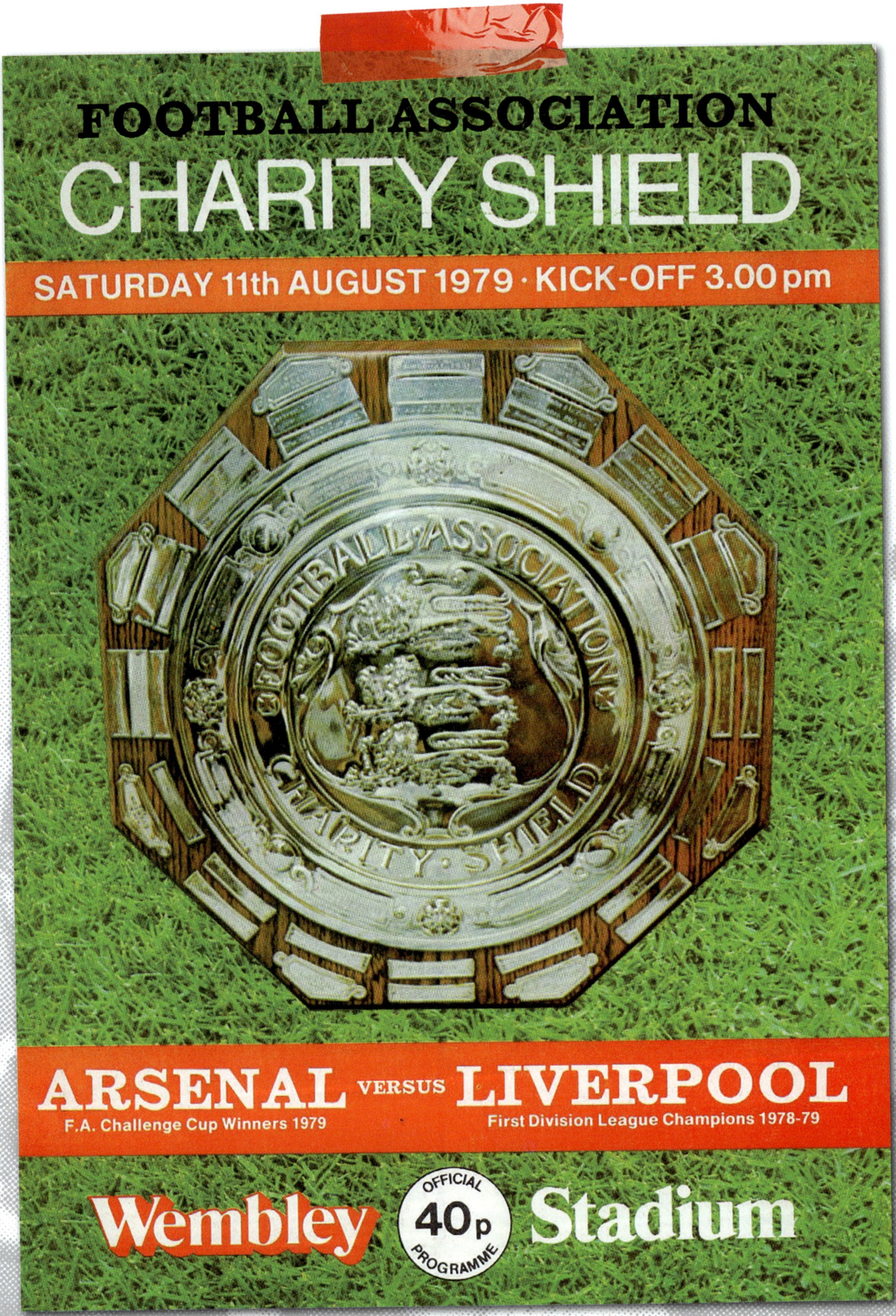


WEMBLEY STADIUM FA CHARITY SHIELD. LIVERPOOL V WEST HAM. LIVERPOOL WITH CHARITY SHIELD 9TH AUG 1980

**What was in store as the 80s approached?**

**The answer, incredibly, was more of the same. Five more years of spectacular success.**

The 1979/80 season became a dash for the top of the Football League between Liverpool and Manchester United. Liverpool lost out in all the Cup games losing 0-1 Arsenal in the third FA Cup semi-final replay. Liverpool clinched the title with a 4-0 win against Aston Villa which was just as well as they lost their final game of the season against Middlesbrough, 1-0.

Having won the title twice in successive seasons a wave of injuries made life difficult for them in the 1980/81 season and they finished fifth in the League, which was their worst placing in a decade.

Their unbeaten home run of 85 matches came to an end against Leicester on the 31st January 1981 and Everton knocked them out of the FA Cup. The fact that Kenny Dalglish only scored eight goals in the League that season showed the size of the problem. Yet Liverpool powered through the European Cup

FA CHARITY SHIELD FOOTBALL
LIVERPOOL V ARSENAL 11TH AUGUST 1979

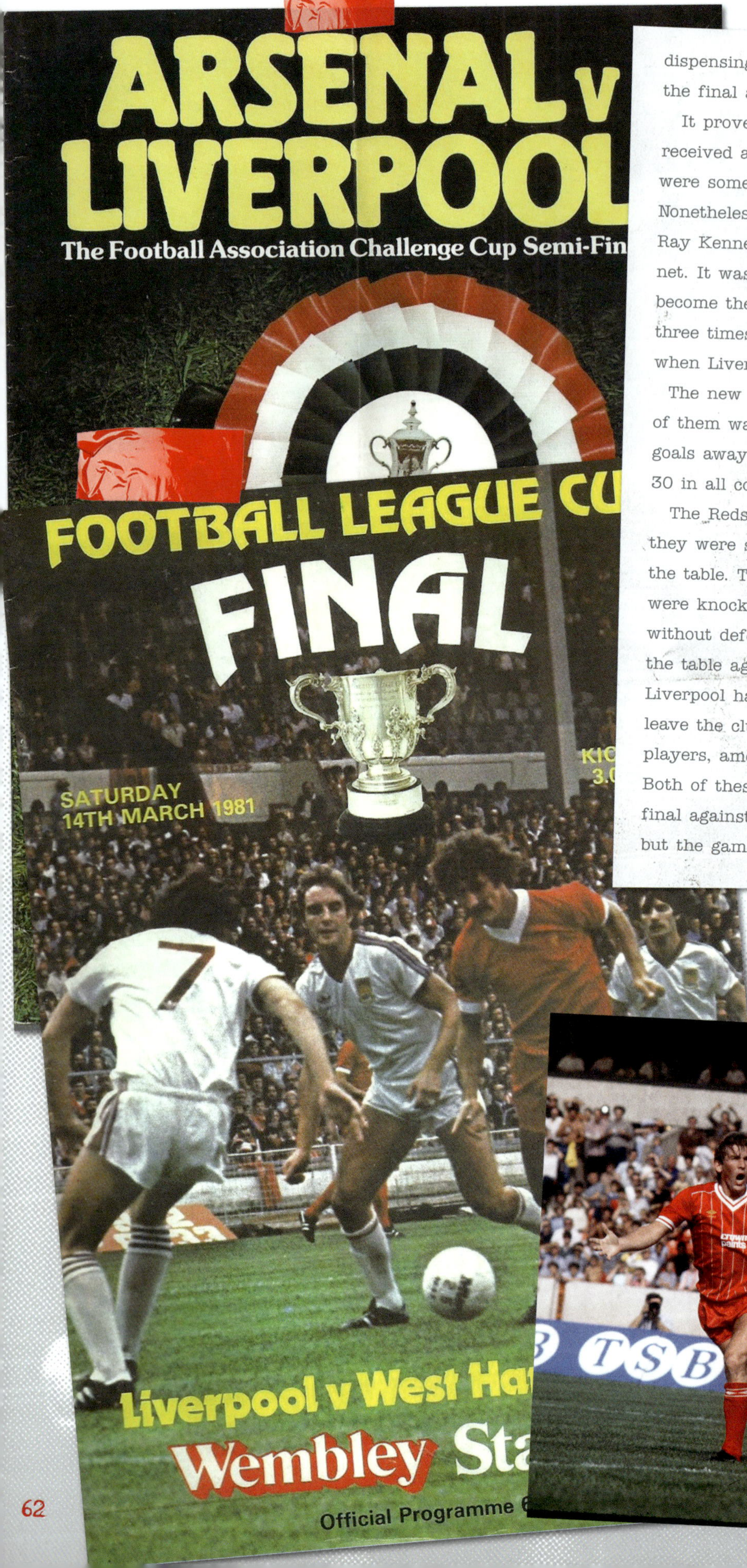


dispensing with Bayern Munich along the way to reach the final against Real Madrid.

It proved to be a tough match. Graeme Souness received an injury shortly after the kick-off and there were some very hard tackles against the Liverpool team. Nonetheless, Liverpool held on and were rewarded by a Ray Kennedy eighty-first-minute drive into the Spanish net. It was enough to win the match. Liverpool had become the first British club to lift the European Cup three times. There was also a League cup to be proud of when Liverpool beat West Ham united 2-1 in the replay.

The new season of 1981/82 was to bring changes. One of them was that Ian Rush suddenly started putting the goals away and became top goalscorer of the season with 30 in all competitions!

The Reds had got off to a bad start and by October they were struggling to get out of the bottom half of the table. The European Cup dream was over when they were knocked out by CSKA Sofia. But a 16-game run without defeat in 1982 saw the Reds rise to the top of the table again. This was quite an achievement because Liverpool had seen both Ray Clemence and Ray Kennedy leave the club and Paisley placed his faith in 5 young players, amongst them Ian Rush and Ronnie Whelan. Both of these young players scored in the League Cup final against Spurs. An early goal put the Reds behind but the game finished 3-1 in Liverpool's favour. Another

KENNY DALGLISH WOLVES V LIVERPOOL 27TH AUG 1983

season, another double to keep the fans happy.

And then came the managerial bombshell, when Paisley announced that the 1982/83 season would be his last.

There was to be no hesitant start to that final season. Liverpool went eight League games without defeat before they slipped up against Ipswich town 1-0. In November they followed a 5-0 victory over HJK Helsinki with another 5-0 thrashing of Everton. Ian Rush was scintillating scoring the only goal up to half time. 6 minutes into the 2nd half Rush put in another before Lawrenson scored Liverpool's third. Rush then scored his hat trick from a rebound off the post before finishing with a run from the halfway line to dodge around the keeper and score his 4th. He repeated his hat-trick magic in a 4-1 win against Coventry a week later.

This was a powerful Liverpool side, which can be seen from the fact that they won the League eleven points clear of second-placed Watford even though they lost five of their final six matches. This was the third time that Liverpool had won the title for two seasons in succession. They added the title to the Football League Cup, which they had won against Manchester United at Wembley 2-1.

They went into the 1983/84 season with some trepidation as they were now without Bob Paisley who had been replaced with 'smokin'' Joe Fagan.

BRUCE GROBBELAAR COMMANDS A TIGHT DEFENCE. 1ST JAN 1986

Liverpool began their matches with a six-game undefeated run to put supporters' minds at rest about the quality of the team under Fagan. They need not have worried for this season was to prove even more spectacular than the last. Ian Rush was on top form and finished the season with 47 goals in all competitions. The Reds thundered five past Odense Boldklub in the European Cup first round and followed it up with a 3-0 win over Everton. On the 26th November in a 1-1 draw against Ipswich Town, Kenny Dalglish scored his 100th league goal for Liverpool with a fantastic drive into the corner of the net. Another eight games without defeat followed including a 4-0 victory over Newcastle United in the third round of the FA Cup.

Disaster struck in the New Year when Kenny Dalglish's cheekbone was smashed in an aerial challenge against Kevin Moran of Manchester United. Violence threatened to break out on the pitch and Graeme Souness had to be restrained by Joe Fagan when he confronted Moran. Dalglish could not play for two months.

Liverpool's League Cup run was also going well. Ian Rush was becoming unstoppable scoring two goals in their 3-0 win over Sheffield Wednesday in a fifth round replay. His hat trick at Villa Park was perhaps the greatest of his career. Liverpool were 1-0 down at the half-time whistle.

# Night of glory as Liverpool triumph ROME

Hardly had the game got underway again when Rush struck with a drive into the net from the edge of the box, which he followed up with a volley from his left foot 15 minutes into the half, chipping in his third over the head of the goalkeeper ten minutes later. 3-1 to the Reds.

After a shock defeat to Walsall in the FA Cup there was another wobble in the League Cup semi-final 2-2 draw against Walsall but the Reds managed to come up with the goods at Fellows Park winning 2-0.

The League Cup final was one to savour as it drew Liverpool against Everton. So when Liverpool won the replay 1-0 the delight was even greater. Now on a roll, Liverpool went into the European Cup semi-final with Dinamo Bucharest and 3-1 on aggregate. It was a miracle they survived the encounter. Emlyn Hughes' opinion was that he had never seen such a dirty team in the European competition.

When Liverpool beat Coventry 5-0 on the 7th May they went five points clear at the top of the League. This was an historic match for Ian Rush. Not only did he score four of the goals, with the last goal he became the first player in six years to score 30 goals in the First Division. With 32 goals in the League he was top goalscorer that year in the First Division.

When Liverpool drew 0-0 with Notts County they secured an historic third consecutive League title. On the crest of a wave, the Reds rolled on to the European Cup final against AS Roma.

Joe Fagan's words to the team were *"If we play, there's nothing in this for them."* Either he was not quite right or Roma played well because after extra time the score was 1-1 and a nerve-wracking penalty shootout began.

Keeper Grobbelaar was on great form stopping two of Roma's four kicks. When Nichols missed Liverpool's first penalty the fans could barely watch. But Neal, Souness, Rush and Kennedy made it four for the Reds and the European Cup was back in Liverpool. An incredible end to an incredible season.

# SWEET ROME

LIVERPOOL LINEUP EUROPEAN CUP FINAL 1984
LIVERPOOL V ROMA 30TH MAY 1984

the olympic stadium, rome, italy
EUROPEAN CUP FINAL
the official uefa souvenir programme £1.50
LIVERPOOL FOOTBALL CLUB
as roma
wednesday 30th may 1984

THE EUROPEAN CUP FINAL 1984 PENALTY SHOOT-OUT LIVERPOOL V ROMA LIVERPOOL WIN ON PENALTIES (4-2) 30TH MAY 1984

LIVERPOOL PLAYERS AND COACHING STAFF CELEBRATE WITH THE EUROPEAN CUP 30TH MAY 1984

Graeme Souness left the club for Italy before the new season. This transfer of such a key player seemed to take the edge off the sparkle slightly in the 1984/5 season. A 1-0 defeat to Everton in the Charity Shield before the season began showed the way forward. Even though they finished second in the League table, there were no trophies to compensate. Liverpool made it through to the European Cup final against Juventus, but lost 1-0 to a penalty that should not have been awarded. A penalty that should have been given to Liverpool was ignored. But the match will be remembered for a terrible reason; a crowd of supporters in the Liverpool section of the stand charged Juventus fans. Crash barriers gave way and a wall collapsed blocking everyone's escape. 39 people died, most of them Italian.

**It was a sad day for Liverpool in another way. Joe Fagan had decided to call it a day at 62.**

**The fans began to wonder whether the glory years were over.**

The club chairman spoke to the next candidate for the job of Liverpool manager. It was Kenny Dalglish. Amazed, Dalglish accepted the job with the proviso that Bob Paisley would be there to guide him for the first two years.

Dalglish's tenure as manager got off to a good start with a 2-0 defeat of Arsenal. Liverpool suffered only two defeats in twenty League matches and had the pleasure of beating Everton 3-2 at Goodison Park. By March of 1985 Liverpool had made good the ten points they had lagged behind Manchester United and after a 2-0 win against Manchester City went to the top of the table.

With the same number of points and a game in hand but one goal less, Everton were on their heels. With 5 goals put past each of Coventry City and Birmingham City along the way, Liverpool finished a great eleven-game run without defeat to finish top of the table, two points clear of Everton. Any doubts about Dalglish's abilities as a manager had long since been silenced.

And now there was FA Cup glory to be looked forward to as well in the final against Everton. Liverpool swept their rivals from the field 3-1 to become just the third team in the 20th century to take both the League and the

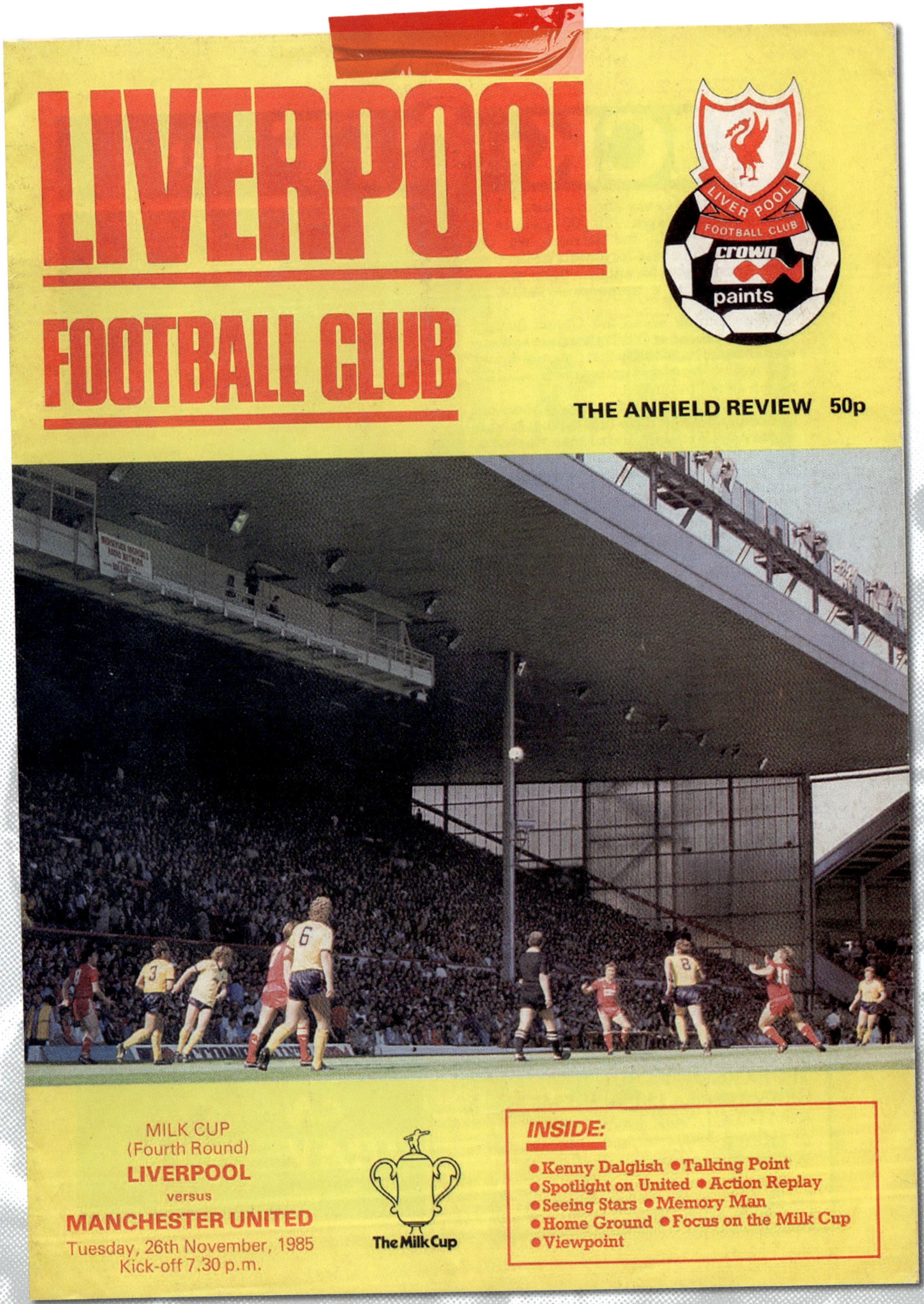
LIVERPOOL
FOOTBALL CLUB
LIVER POOL
FOOTBALL CLUB
crown
paints
THE ANFIELD REVIEW 50p
MILK CUP
(Fourth Round)
LIVERPOOL
versus
MANCHESTER UNITED
Tuesday, 26th November, 1985
Kick-off 7.30 p.m.
The Milk Cup
INSIDE:
• Kenny Dalglish • Talking Point
• Spotlight on United • Action Replay
• Seeing Stars • Memory Man
• Home Ground • Focus on the Milk Cup
• Viewpoint

JOHN ALDRIDGE CELEBRATES AFTER SCORING AGAINST ARSENAL 15 AUGUST 1987

FA Cups in the same season.

This incredible season was followed by another drought. Ian Rush scored 14 goals in all competitions and Liverpool were unable to lift any trophies; what was even more galling was coming second to Everton in the League having thrown away three games in succession. Dalglish took responsibility for this dry season saying that he had wanted to buy four new players but as this took longer than he had anticipated, he had decided to wait.

Ian Rush had already decided to leave the club at the end of the 1986/87 season and left for Italy. Over the summer, John Barnes arrived from Watford and Peter Beardsley from Newcastle.

**Dalglish had formed a strong team with an adventurous spirit.**

29 League games without defeat in the new season was an incredible, unmatched achievement brought to a halt only by Everton who got revenge for their FA Cup

JOHN BARNES PERFORMS AN OVERHEAD KICK ABOVE DAVID O'LEARY OF ARSENAL AUGUST 1987

JOHN BARNES CELEBRATES THE WINNING GOAL WITH IAN RUSH 20TH MAY 1989

final defeat with a 1-0 victory over the Reds. With Beardsley, Barnes and the other new signing John Aldridge popping in the goals (until the defeat at Everton the Reds scored 67) Liverpool powered to the top of the table and when they beat Tottenham 1-0, they secured the title with four games still to play. It seemed unbelievable, then, when they lost 1-0 to Wimbledon in the FA Cup final.

Lawrenson retired before the next season started. But there was an announcement to shock the fans just as the 1988/89 season was getting underway. Ian Rush had returned to Liverpool. Dalglish now had Barnes, Aldridge, Beardsley and Rush to score goals. Perhaps this was one goalscorer too many?

With only one win to show after a run of six matches, which included a 3-1 defeat to Manchester United on the 1st January 1989, Dalglish read the riot act to his team. It did the trick with Liverpool winning fifteen of their next eighteen League games and they drew the other three.

And then Liverpool were again caught up in a stadium disaster. In their FA Cup semi-final tie against Nottingham Forest on the 15th April 1989 police had tried to ease congestion amongst the supporters by opening gates to the central pens of the ground. The crush that resulted left ninety-four people dead on the day. Two more died in hospital and 766 other people were injured. All of them were Liverpool supporters. Kenny Dalglish was a central figure at the club during these difficult times, often weighed down with emotion during the numerous funerals that he attended.

Despite the horror and the difficult days that followed, Liverpool did not let the chance of another FA Cup final victory against Everton pass them by. And it was Ian Rush who scored the winning two goals to give Dalglish his second FA Cup. Liverpool were pipped at the post when Arsenal won the League with both teams on 76 points but Arsenal won, just one goal ahead. Three important games in six days had taken their toll.

Ian Rush was given a permanent place in the team in the 1989/90 season and Aldridge was sidelined, which caused him great hurt. But the team started out on an eight-match, undefeated run; it included a 9-0 thrashing of Crystal Palace that broke Liverpool's record for the most goals in a First Division match.

They tripped up in November losing four out of five matches but regained their momentum, and despite losing 3-4 to Crystal Palace later in the season, they finished in a powerful blaze pushing four past Charlton athletic and Chelsea and beating Coventry 6-1 in the final match of the season. That game took the team nine points clear of Aston Villa to take the league title.

That made two trophies, as Liverpool had also won the Charity Shield 1-0 against Arsenal.

**BUT THE END OF THE SEASON HERALDED SOMETHING FAR LESS CHEERFUL; A DECLINE.**

# REDS ON THE RUN!

## HAVE LIVERPOOL LOST THE FEAR FACTOR?

RONNIE MORAN, KENNY DALGLISH AND ROY EVANS CELEBRATE THE CHAMPIONSHIP WIN WITH THE TROPHIES 1ST MAY 1990

SQUAD CELEBRATE AFTER WINNING THE CHAMPIONSHIP 28TH APRIL 1990

# WHERE HAVE ALL THE TROPHIES GONE?

The glorious years of triumphs that had taken Liverpool through from 1973 were coming to an end. This was the last time they would win two trophies until 2001.

Only the Charity Shield came their way the next season, and even that was a draw, 1-1, against Manchester United. Liverpool were saved by a John Barnes' penalty kick.

When Kenny Dalglish resigned in 1991 blaming, in part, the aftermath of the Hillsborough disaster for his decision, the Reds had seen almost twenty years filled with titles and trophies.

They were now on the edge of a drought. There was, though, one more triumph to celebrate before the fans were to be left thirsty.

**When Graeme Souness took over the helm, everyone was hopeful of a resurgence, it was not be.**

It wasn't a good season in the league; ten defeats do not champions make. Add 16 drawn matches and an abysmal second half to a season and what do you get? Miraculously, 6th place.

So to the FA Cup. Brushing over the fact the opposition en route was not exactly top notch – Aston Villa was the only team in League Division 1 – at least the competition ended successfully for the lads in red; 2-0 against Sunderland.

Souness was proving to be less than successful and that cup was the only honour that Liverpool would bring home under his management. League results were dismal and the writing had been emblazoned on the wall long before Souness was dismissed in January 1994; but the rot continued and Liverpool finished on 8th position.

One of the bright spots in the Liverpool story at this time was Michael Owen. The brilliant forward, who won accolades from all sides and had been called, "the best attacker of his age in the country" became top goalscorer for the club for every year between 1997 and 2004, scoring 118 goals in his

## LIVERPOOL
## FA CUP WINNERS 1991/92

LIVERPOOL CELEBRATE THEIR WIN AGAINST SUNDERLAND WITH THE FA CUP TROPHY 9TH MAY 1992

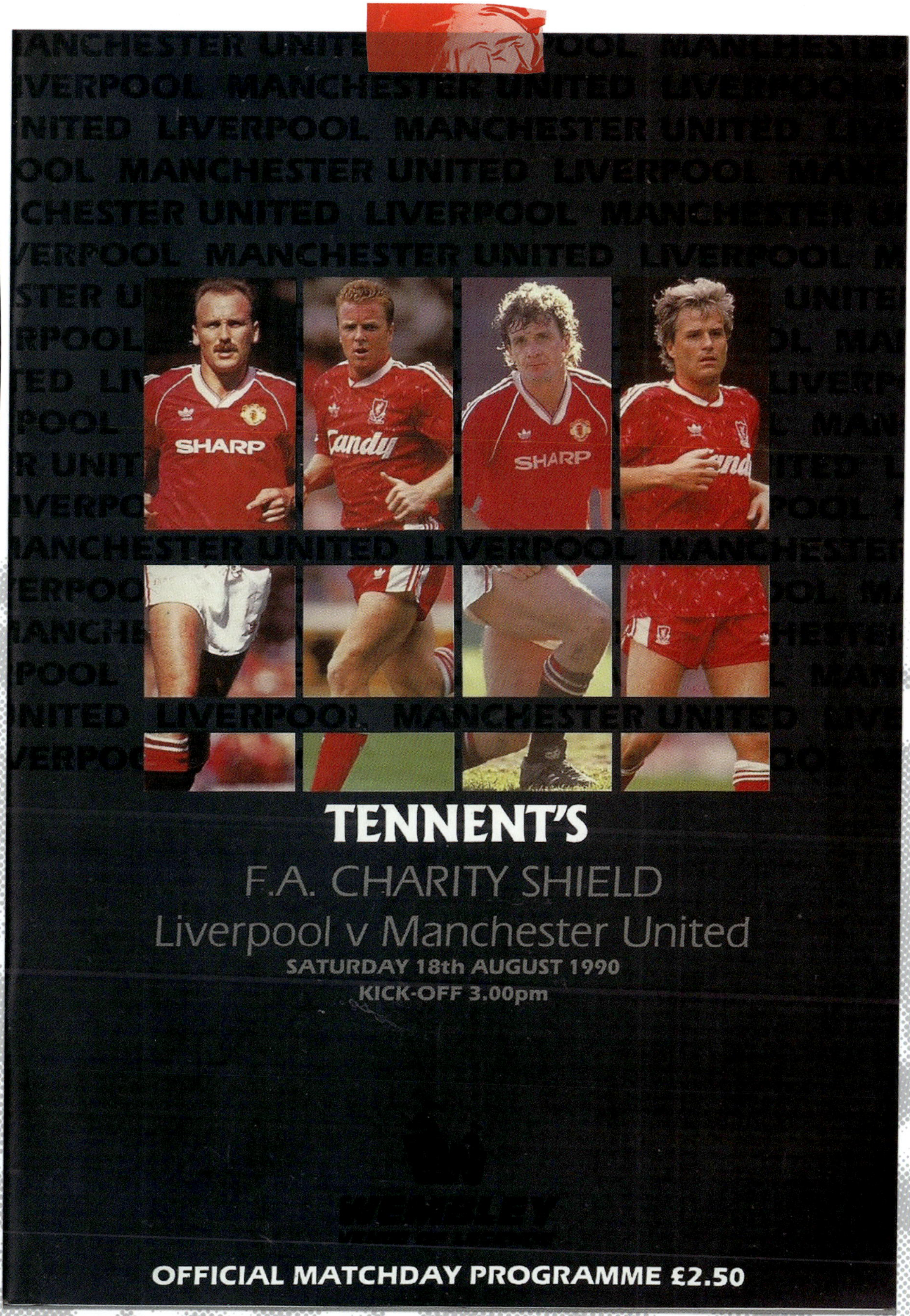

LIVERPOOL FOOTBALL CLUB P.L.C.
Carlsberg
LIVERPOOL
RED SEATS
F.A. PREMIER LEAGUE
LIVERPOOL V SOUTHAMPTON
TUE 01 SEP 1992 KO 07:30 P.M.
ANFIELD ROAD
AREA AR
ROW 9
SEAT 96
PRICE 12.00
Enter via VISITORS 61-66
MATCH INFORMATION SERVICE
MATCH TICKET OFFICE ENQUIRIES
TO BE RETAINED

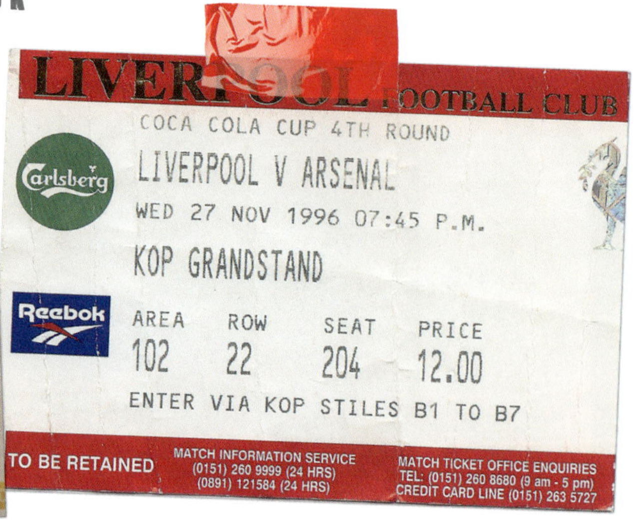
LIVERPOOL FOOTBALL CLUB
COCA COLA CUP 4TH ROUND
Carlsberg
LIVERPOOL V ARSENAL
WED 27 NOV 1996 07:45 P.M.
KOP GRANDSTAND
Reebok
AREA 102
ROW 22
SEAT 204
PRICE 12.00
ENTER VIA KOP STILES B1 TO B7
TO BE RETAINED
MATCH INFORMATION SERVICE
(0151) 260 9999 (24 HRS)
(0891) 121584 (24 HRS)
MATCH TICKET OFFICE ENQUIRIES
TEL: (0151) 260 8680 (9 am - 5 pm)
CREDIT CARD LINE (0151) 263 5727

years at Liverpool.

Roy Evans had taken over what by now might have seemed to be a poisoned chalice. While he was unable to get the team's league form back into balance, he did, at least, help get them through to the League Cup Final in 1995, which they won 2-1, against Bolton Wanderers. But he couldn't bring about the change that was so badly needed, and for the next five, challenging years, Liverpool failed to make the grade in any competition. The best they could do was 3rd and the worst was 7th in the league, which is where they ended when Frenchman Gérard Houllier was brought in as co-manager in the 1998/99 season. Evans resigned leaving Houllier in sole charge for the 1999/2000 season. What could he do? At least Steven George Gerrard was still there to delight the hearts of fans. But Tony Warner, Paul Ince, Steve Harkness, Jason McAteer, David James and Rob Jones and Steve McManaman all left the club. It was not a summer designed to inspire confidence. Neither were four losses at home: to Watford, Manchester United, Everton and Leicester City, which was the worst at 2-0.

## What hope for 2000/01, then?

Well, fast forward to the end of the season. In the league, a spate of five defeats in nine games hobbled the team early on, and they bounced around between third and sixth before settling on third position at the end.

But elsewhere, an extraordinary turn around had taken place. Liverpool were proud holders of a triple; the FA Cup, the League Cup and the UEFA Cup. In the FA Cup, Arsenal had fallen foul of them, 2-1 and in the League it was the turn of Birmingham City, although it was justice that they were beaten 5-4 on penalties after they had snatched a draw at full time after a penalty on the 90th minute.

And then there was international glory in the UEFA Cup, too, when Liverpool dispensed with such illustrious names as Porto and Barcelona on the way

MICHAEL OWEN SCORES THE FIRST GOAL DURING THE AXA SPONSORED 2001 FA CUP FINAL AGAINST ARSENAL 12TH MAY 2001

↑ LIVERPOOL CELEBRATE WINNING THE AXA SPONSORED 2001 FA CUP FINAL AGAINST ARSENAL 12TH MAY 2001

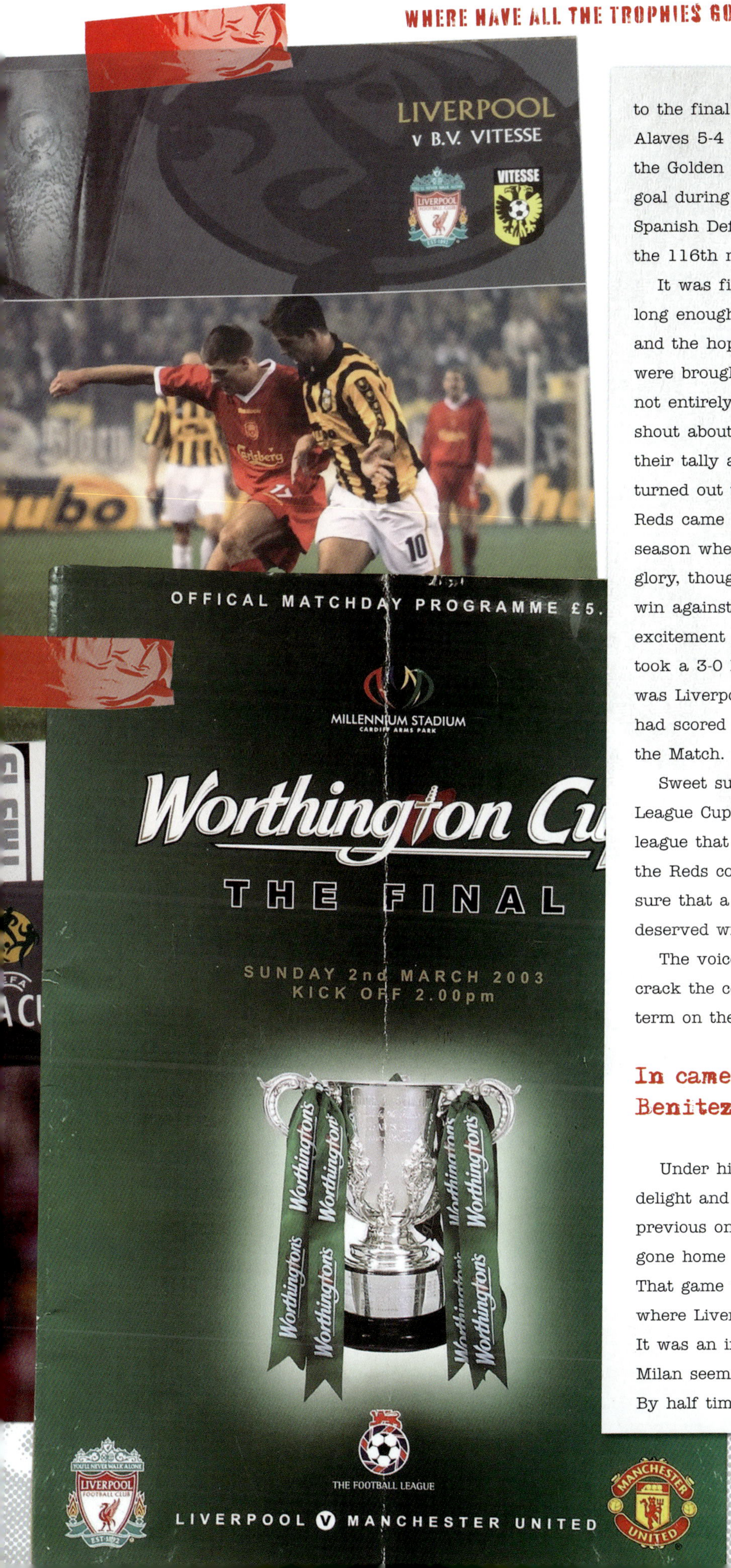


to the final. In the final they trumped Spanish club Alaves 5-4 in an electrifying match. Liverpool won under the Golden Goal rule, whereby the team that scored a goal during extra time was the winner. And it was the Spanish Defender Delfí Geli who scored an own goal on the 116th minute and gave Liverpool the cup!

It was fitting, too, that Michael Owen had stayed long enough to enjoy those three moments of wonder, and the hope that this revival would prove permanent were brought into the 2001/02 season. And although not entirely fulfilled, there was certainly enough to shout about, because they added the Charity Shield to their tally at Manchester United's expense; 2-1. Which turned out to be good omen for the league where the Reds came 2nd, their best position since the 1990/91 season when they had also been second. The greater glory, though came in the 2001 and a UEFA Super Cup win against German super club Bayern Munich, 2-3. The excitement was almost beyond bearing when Liverpool took a 3-0 lead only for Bayern to pull back two. But it was Liverpool's day and that man Michael Owen, who had scored the third goal, was singled out as the Man of the Match.

Sweet success against Manchester United in the League Cup Final made up for the lack of success in the league that season of 2002/03 when 5th was the best the Reds could do. Wonder kids Owen and Gerrard made sure that a 2-0 win proved that their team was the deserved winner.

The voices of discontent at Liverpool's inability to crack the code in the league brought an end to Houllier's term on the 24th of May 2004.

**In came the Valencia coach Rafael Benitez to see what he could do.**

Under his watchful eye, there was another game to delight and thrill fans in the 2004/05 season after the previous one had proved disappointing and fans had gone home without any titles or cups to cheer them. That game was the 2005 UEFA Champions League Final where Liverpool lined up against the mighty Milan. It was an incredible Liverpool performance. And yet Milan seemed, at first, to be burying the English club. By half time they were 3-0 down and it seemed an impossible task lay ahead of them. But the team were inspired when they returned to the pitch and it took just nine minutes before the fight back took shape. Gerrard started it with his 54th minute goal and two minutes later Šmicer had shocked the entire stadium with number two. Just four minutes later Alonso stunned the Italians with his 60th minute strike. Now there was nothing to separate them. Except during the penalty shoot out. Liverpool kept their nerve and the Italians went down 2-3.

It was the Reds' fifth European Cup title, so Liverpool were awarded the trophy permanently, and were awarded the UEFA Badge of Honour.

From this high point, Liverpool went on to prove that they were still a top force by winning two more trophies the following season 2005/06: the UEFA Super Cup and the FA Cup. They were third in the league; was Benítez the saviour they had been looking for?

When Benítez steered them home to third place again in 2006/07, it seemed as though he was on the right track, although the only silverware came in the form of the Community Shield (the Charity Shield had changed its name in 2002), where Liverpool beat Chelsea 2-1. Liverpool even, finally, made a determined challenge for the league title in 2008/09, a great season when they lost just two games and enjoyed a fifteen-game undefeated run. Manchester United were crushed 4-1 in Manchester, and Chelsea went down twice. How bitter to see that very United team take the championship. But this was a team to build on for the future.

Ah, no. Benítez, in fact, was the unwelcome herald of a period of such parched hopes as had not been experienced since the dreadful 1947 season began in the days of Billy Liddell. In nine seasons, just one trophy would materialise: the League Cup in 2012 against Cardiff. Once again, Liverpool had scraped past in a 2-3 penalty shoot out (Gerrard failed to score) after the teams had reached the end of extra time at 2-2.

The league performances were dismal for a team of their stature with 7th, 6th, 8th and 7th position in four consecutive seasons. By 2010/11. Liverpool had a new manager, Roy Hodgson and was practically bankrupt. New owners took over; the Fenway Sports Group. They lasted longer than Hodgson who was already gone by the summer of 2011.

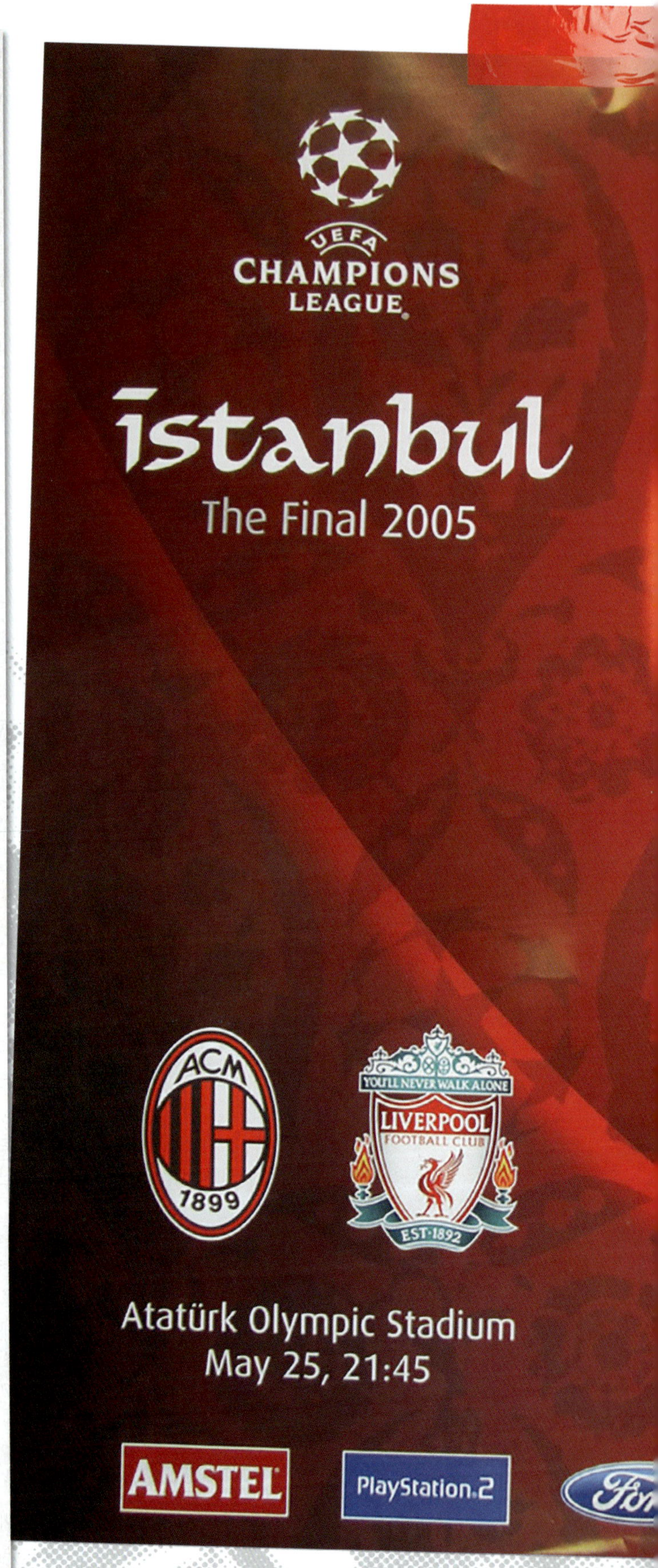

STEVEN GERRARD CELEBRATES WITH THE TROPHY AFTER HIS TEAM BEAT CARDIFF CITY TO WIN THE LEAGUE CUP FINAL AT WEMBLEY STADIUM IN LONDON, ON FEBRUARY 26, 2012

# GERRARD FA

Now the uncertainty on the pitch was replaced with a revolving door of confusion off the pitch which wreaked havoc amongst the players. The directors now looked to a man to take over who had done wonders in the past; Kenny Dalglish. They got an eighth wonder, that record eighth League Cup win, to balance out the eighth place in the league table, the worst result in 18 years.

**Weighing up the results, the directors decided that Dalglish had to go.**

The fans were longing for a man of steel. They got Brendan Rodgers. Not quite good enough for Liverpool. They finished 7th. And lived to tell the tale.

But at least he managed to make the squad challengers for the league title in 2013/14. And they scored the second highest number of goals ever; 101. A shame then that all that effort led nowhere. They came so close, let down by one poor performance at home against Southampton early in the season, losing 0-1. With glorious consistency they played 16 games without defeat and topped the table in the home run only to stumble against Chelsea in the third last game of the season, 0-2 at home. They finished in second place just two points behind Manchester City. It was a bitter disappointment without any other honours to celebrate. But Rodgers had no more answers and the following two seasons saw the Reds far away from the big boys. 6th in 2015.

For one Liverpool legend, Steven Gerrard, it was time to call it a day at Liverpool. The day fans had dreaded was the 16th of May when he played his last game in front of the home crowd. 8 days later his last game and goal were watched by fans at Stoke.

By the time, the 2015/16 had got underway the directors had seen all they wanted to; in October he was given his marching orders. By the 8th of November, the

STEVEN GERRARD APPLAUDS THE FANS AFTER HIS LAST GAME AGAINST STOKE CITY AT BRITANNIA STADIUM 24TH MAY 2015

# EWELL TO KOP

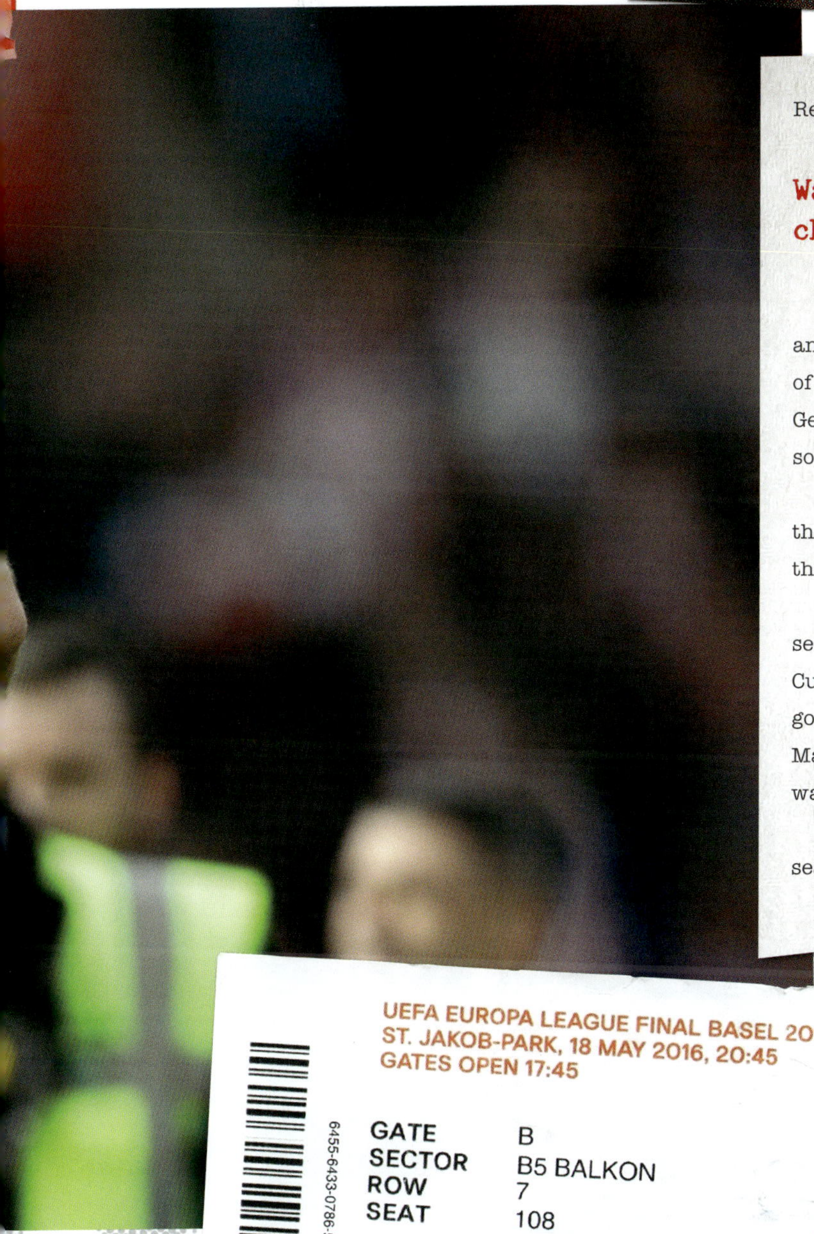

Reds had won just four of their twelve games.

## Was there no one who could bring cheer back to the Kop?

It was time for a high profile man to take charge and the man chosen was Jürgen Klopp, the manager of German team Borussia Dortmund. Klopp had been German Football Manager of the Year in 2011 and 2012, so here was someone with teeth and results.

Yet not even he was able to piece together a team that could do anything but limp to eighth place again by the summer of 2016.

But the young shoots of revival could already be seen; in February of 2016, the Reds lost in the League Cup final to Manchester City on penalties, 1-3. And they got to the final of the UEFA Europa League taking out Manchester United and Borussia Dortmund along the way, but were beaten by Seville, 3-1.

And the young shoots grew stronger as the 2016/17 season ripened.

With a 4-3 away win over Arsenal, Liverpool were

back in the thick of it. They soon had an eleven game unbeaten run under their belts suffering just two losses, and had hit top spot before entering the new year on 2nd place. This was a reinvigorated side with new confidence capable of taking down high-flying Chelsea 2-1, Watford by a whacking 6-1 and Manchester City were taken down, albeit by a single goal.

Unfortunately... then came the fateful January of 2017. 7 games with three losses and the FA Cup run ended with a 2-1 defeat at home to Wolverhampton.

Swansea City, 2-3, Hull City, 2-0 and Leicester City, 3-1, put the boot in and the Reds lost valuable ground on the league leaders. Happily, Klopp steadied the boat after that, and a modest 7-game undefeated run followed. In fact there was only one more defeat until the end of the season, 2-1, although, aggravatingly that was at home to Crystal Palace.

But the lads never gave up and fought back again to beat Watford 1-0 at Watford and West Ham 4-0 at West Ham, finishing the season in style with a 3-0 thumping of Middlesbrough.

**So, no silverware in 2017, but a team spirit that brought hope and a 4th place in the Premiership.**

Phillipe Coutinho emerged as the top goalscorer with 14, just pipping Sadio Mané to the honour with his EFL goal.

Klopp had achieved an impressive amount and proven that Liverpool could land the punches to get to the top. There was hard work ahead and the manager was on the look-out for several more players to strengthen the squad and resolve the weaknesses. Still, the manager had already turned the team's fortunes and the fans hopes around. The drama and excitement under his guidance was only just beginning.

One of those recruited by Klopp at the tail end of the 2017 season was Egyptian forward Mohamed Salah Hamed Mahrous Ghaly, one of the world's best and a sign that Klopp was serious about bringing Liverpool back to the top. Salah would repay the trust placed in him by becoming the season's top goalscorer for the club with a total of 44 in all games.

As the 2018 season got underway, early signs were that not all the holes had been plugged. 3 wins from 9 games was not the start the team had hoped for and a crashing defeat to Manchester City, 5-0, two home draws and an away defeat to Tottenham set the points for the season, which a run of 14 games without defeat could not change.

September proved challenging. Having beaten Hoffenheim 6-3 on aggregate in August, on the 13th of September, Liverpool started out in the UEFA Champions League group stage playing Sevilla at home. Following a mistake by Dejan Lovren, Sevilla scored the first goal after just 5 minutes.

Liverpool recovered and fought back hard to be

rewarded with a 21st-minute goal by Firmino, who was followed in the 37th minute by Salah. A missed penalty by Firmino in the 41st minute and another Sevilla goal saw the game end in a disappointing 2-2 draw.

Neither was there any comfort from the EFL third round when they lost 2-0 to Leicester in September, and struggled to get their 3-2 revenge in the league later in the month.

Over the winter months, the UEFA Cup began to produce the kind of results that Liverpool needed with 7 goals knocked past both Maribor and Spartak

DANIEL STURRIDGE CELEBRATES AFTER SCORING DURING THE UEFA EUROPA LEAGUE FINAL AGAINST SEVILLA IN BASEL 18TH MAY 2016

Moscow. Once Sevilla was out of the way after a 3-3 draw, they were into the round of 16.

Another 3 home draws rather dampened the 4-3 league success in January 2018 against Manchester City as did being kicked out of the FA Cup 4th round by West Brom. From that point in the season, 8 wins from 15 games were not going to be enough to catch Manchester City, who were sailing towards the championship with 100 points. A 2-0 defeat in Manchester against United condemned Liverpool to a final 4th place for the second year in row and hammering in 5 against Watford, although it was something to cheer about ushered in just 3 wins from the last 7 games.

There was more to cheer about in the UEFA Cup. The Reds thrashed Porto 5-0 on aggregate and revenge was sweet when they met Manchester City in the quarter-finals and downed them in both legs, 3-0 and 2-1 with Salah and Mané striking home on both occasions.

Liverpool really showed what they were capable of in the semi-final against Roma, scoring a 5-2 victory in April and a magnificent Salah hat-trick, although they left fans with their hearts in their mouths during the second leg in May 2018 losing 4-2, so scraping through to the final 6-7 on aggregate. Klopp had brought the team back to within an inch of glory.

PHILIPPE COUTINHO OF LIVERPOOL CELEBRATES HIS GOAL WHICH GAVE HIS TEAM A 2-1 LEAD AGAINST EVERTON 1ST APRIL 2017

Real Madrid, however, proved to be an impossible nut to crack in the final, especially as star player Salah suffered a serious injury just 30 minutes into the game. Even though Mané equalised 5 minutes after Real had gone into the lead, it was not enough and Liverpool lost 3-1. It had been a bad match for keeper Loris Karius, who was later diagnosed as having played suffering from concussion.

**GLORY HAD BEEN TANTALISINGLY CLOSE, AND DESPITE THE LOSS, GAVE IMMENSE HOPE FOR THE FUTURE.**

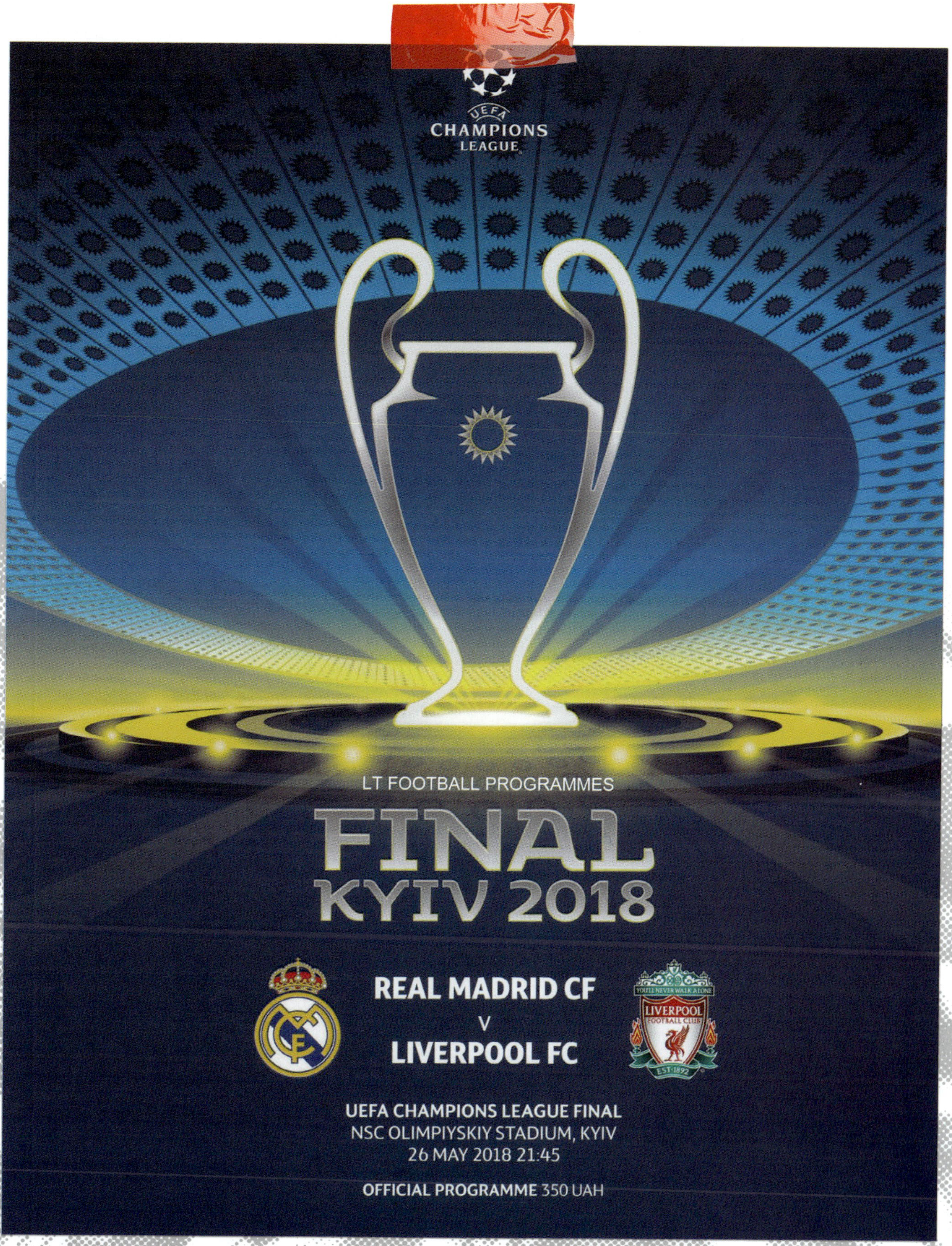
UEFA
CHAMPIONS
LEAGUE
LT FOOTBALL PROGRAMMES
FINAL
KYIV 2018
REAL MADRID CF
V
LIVERPOOL FC
UEFA CHAMPIONS LEAGUE FINAL
NSC OLIMPIYSKIY STADIUM, KYIV
26 MAY 2018 21:45
OFFICIAL PROGRAMME 350 UAH

# KLOPP KLOP

## WHO'S THERE?

The 2018-19 pre-season friendly games produced some interesting results, and along the way both Manchester City and United were defeated. Was this a good omen for the coming 2019 season? Who would be foolish enough to bet money on it. But as it turned out, they would have been right, for Liverpool took off into one of the most successful, thrilling and nail-biting seasons for many a long year, one that fans will remember long into the future. This was the season when Jürgen Klopp's boys struck gold... or rather, glittering silver.

Klopp had signed two midfielders, Naby Keita and Fabinho, forward Xherdan Shaqiri and Brazilian keeper Alisson Becker (what a Godsend he would prove to be!) in the summer transfer window, and between them they would add ten goals to the season's final tally.

Unbeaten in 20 games until the 29th of December 2018, Klopp's boys hurtled to the top of the league reaping some impressive results along the way, taking down Tottenham Hotspur in London 2-1, Watford 3-1, holding Manchester City to a draw at home and then sending Manchester United back home with 3-1 loss to think about. It was the final match of that magic run that

LIV

LIVERPOOL SQUAD POSE FOR A TEAM PHOTO AT ANFIELD ON AUGUST 30, 2018

RPOOL!

really showed the team's class and potential, however, a magnificent 5-1 drubbing of Arsenal. Firmino, Mané and Salah did the damage. Firmino, razor-sharp, took two goals on the 14th and 16th minutes, then added a penalty in the 65th minute to complete his hat trick. This was Liverpool's ninth Premier League win in a row.

Unfortunately, this terrific win seemed to distract the lads, for the following week they went down to Manchester City in Manchester, although only by 2-1. The team was in such good form, that this defeat would not have mattered had it not been for the home draw against Leicester, who they had beaten 1-2 away earlier in the season. That momentary lapse cost them dear.

The Reds went on to produce a thrilling seventeen-game undefeated run to end the season, the last nine all victories, during which Tottenham and Chelsea felt the Klopp whip and both Watford and Huddersfield were thrashed 5-0, Mané taking two on each occasion with one of the season's new boys Naby Keita and the season's top goalscorer Mohamed Salah (27 goals, top goalscorer for the second successive season) also getting in on the goal-scoring act. Sadio Mané was hot on Salah's heels as the season ended with 26 goals to his credit.

All of this was not enough, sadly, to compensate for that one home draw, because when the season ended on May the 12th 2019, the lads had lost the Premiership to Manchester City by one point; 97 to 98. It was heartbreaking after such a magnificent run. As the FA Cup and the EFL Cup had also been barren affairs, there was but one hope of deserved glory left for the team, although it was not going to be easy to transform that hope into reality; the hope was the UEFA Champions League trophy.

Nonetheless, Liverpool had a great chance; they had made it through to the final and fought hard and long to get there, dispensing with some illustrious teams en route. The first tough nuts had been Bayern Munich, who fell badly, however, to the Liverpool steamroller, 3-1 on aggregate. Porto were next and collapsed 6-1 on aggregate leaving the formidable Barcelona with the awesome Lionel Messi to subdue.

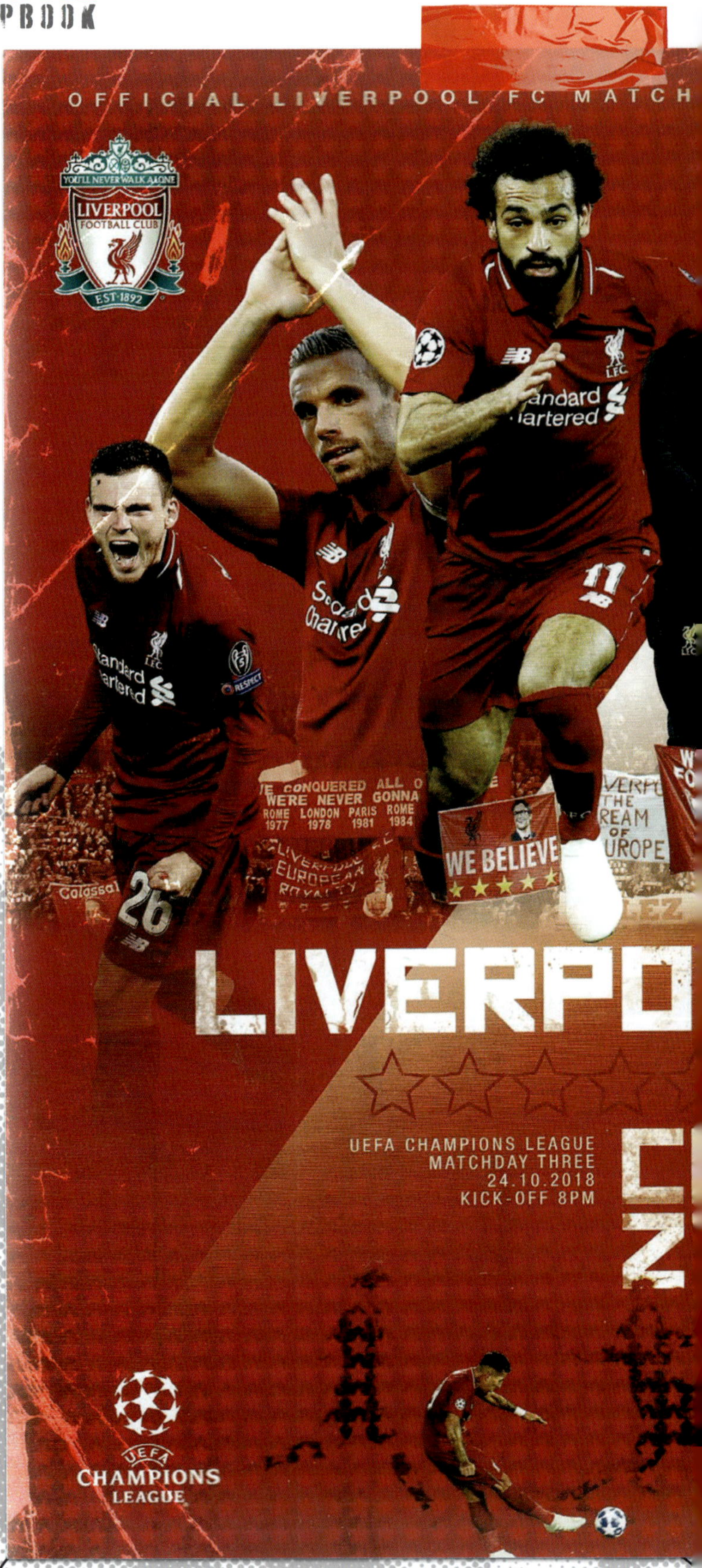


MOHAMED SALAH OF LIVERPOOL WITH DANNY ROSE OF TOTTENHAM HOTSPUR DURING THE PREMIER LEAGUE MATCH BETWEEN LIVERPOOL FC AND TOTTENHAM HOTSPUR AT ANFIELD ON MARCH 31, 2019

SADIO MANE OF LIVERPOOL SCORES THE FIRST GOAL DURING THE PREMIER LEAGUE MATCH BETWEEN LIVERPOOL FC AND CHELSEA FC AT ANFIELD ON APRIL 14, 2019

JORDI ALBA OF BARCELONA & IVAN RAKITIC BATTLE FOR POSSESSION WITH MOHAMED SALAH, DURING THE UEFA CHAMPIONS LEAGUE SEMI FINAL FIRST LEG MATCH, AT THE NOU CAMP ON MAY 01, 2019

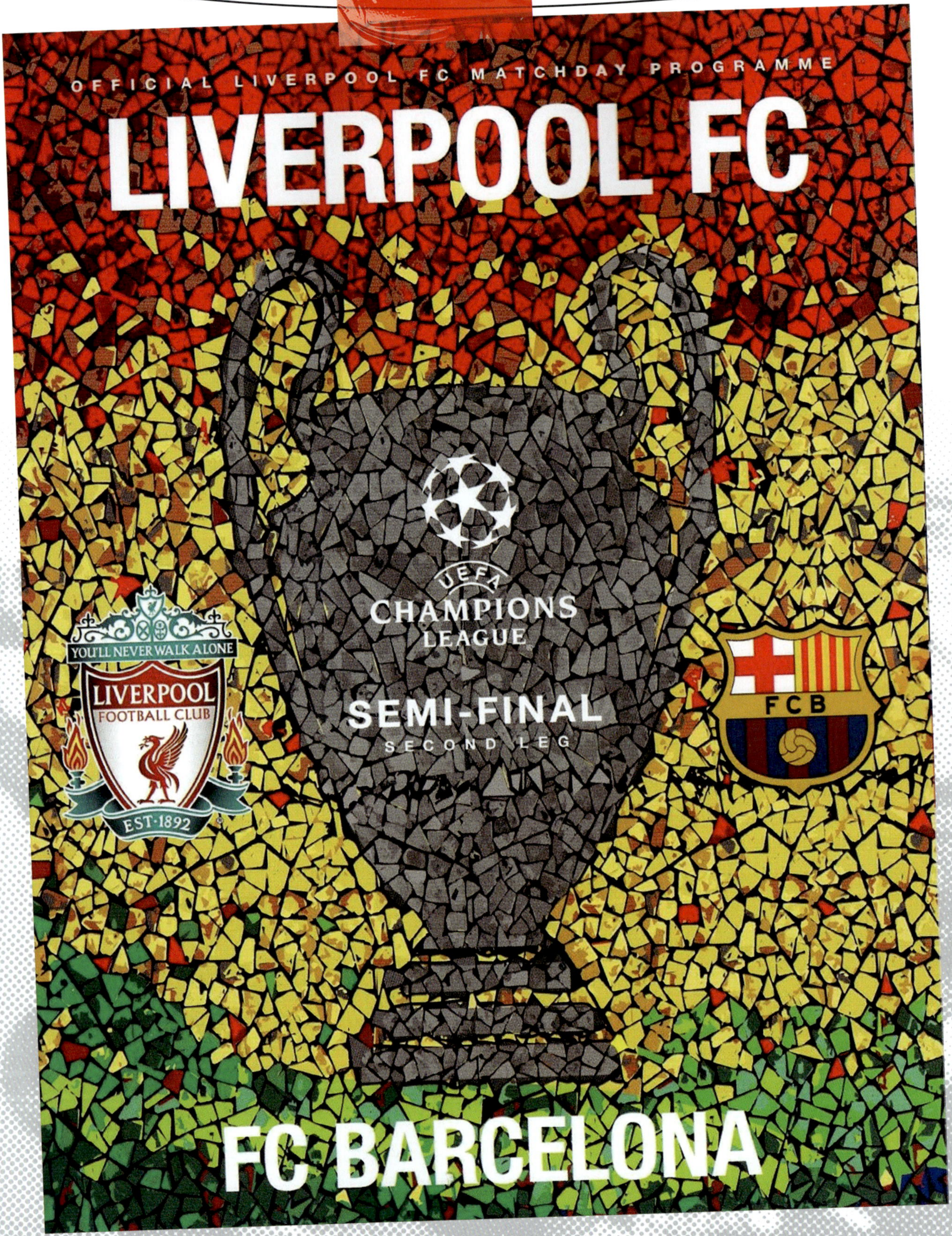

BARCELONA'S LIONEL MESSI UNDER PRESSURE FROM LIVERPOOL'S FABINHO DURING THE UEFA CHAMPIONS LEAGUE SEMI FINAL SECOND LEG, ANFIELD ON MAY 7, 201

In the first round it seemed as though the task was beyond the lads. Barcelona struck three times and Messi twice handing out a 3-0 defeat to the Liverpudlians. Anyone going to sleep that night dreaming that Barcelona would soon be European Champions could have easily been forgiven for their dreams.

The would-be giant killers Liverpool ran out onto the Anfield turf on the 7th May to face the uphill struggle against a super confident Barca - and they were starting the match without Salah and Fermino.

So when Henderson outwitted the Barca defences on the 7th minute and his left-foot strike could not be held by the Barca keeper leaving Divoc Origi to slot in the first goal, you would have needed ear plugs to survive the Liverpool supporters' roar. This was Liverpool's answer to Barca's dreams of supremacy. With the bit between their teeth, Barca were about to experience the Red Devils in full flow.

Barca were fortunate to escape a penalty as the Reds began to harry the Barca defences and Mané was tripped in the area; the referee ignored the foul. Liverpool fought for every ball, giving nothing and overwhelming the Barca game plan. Messi only got in on the act after some 12 minutes with a great drive that Brazilian goalie Alisson's quick reactions neutralised, and again on the 18th minute sending a drive past the post. By then Barca were beginning to find their rhythm, but if they got through the defence then Alisson was impenetrable, lighting-fast either in the air or on the ground.

As the first half wore on and Barca mounted sharp attacks, Klopp's frustration began to show and the hopes of half an hour before were beginning to look threadbare. Nonetheless, the defence held fast and repulsed every yellow threat. With another misdirected shot from Messi, the first half ended. There were now just 45 minutes to climb the mountain that had risen up in front of Liverpool.

Liverpool gave Barca nothing as the second-half minutes ticked away; they were first to the ball, forcing the Barca men into hasty reaction. But how were the Reds going to manage three goals in such a short space of time?

The man who showed them the way was Dutchman Georginio Wijnaldum. When a cross came towards the centre hard and low, he sprinted in on the 54th minute and with a powerful one-touch drive rocketed the ball towards the Barca net leaving the keeper no chance, the ball smashing into his hand on its way into the net. Liverpool were now just one moment away from the recovery of a lifetime. The unthinkable had become possible and the Reds were eager to make this the match of a lifetime.

And how determined they were, because just one minute later, they were back on the attack and Shaquiri sent over a high cross for Wijnaldum to sail up above the defence and head home a bullet that left the Barca keeper immobile and still on his feet. Two for Wijnaldum, three for Liverpool.

Faced with this extraordinary turnaround, the Barcelona train was in danger of running out of steam as Liverpool sensed that they were capable of pulling off the comeback of their dreams.

They did not relent, they kept up the pressure, they

GEORGINIO WIJNALDUM OF LIVERPOOL CELEBRATES AFTER SCORING HIS TEAM'S THIRD GOAL DURING THE UEFA CHAMPIONS LEAGUE SEMI FINAL SECOND LEG MATCH, AT ANFIELD ON MAY 07, 2019

JORDAN HENDERSON OF LIVERPOOL CELEBRATES AFTER THE UEFA CHAMPIONS LEAGUE SEMI FINAL SECOND LEG MATCH BETWEEN LIVERPOOL AND BARCELONA AT ANFIELD ON MAY 07, 2019

swept forward and produced one of the most impudent, brilliant goals the crowd had ever had the pleasure to witness.

It was the 78th minute. Alexander-Arnold feigned leaving a corner kick to a teammate only to dart back and whip the ball into the centre with the accuracy of a laser, where Origi had been left far too much room, and he obliged by driving in his one-touch second goal, swerving the ball away from the keeper into the corner of the net. Now, not even ear plugs would have helped, because the Liverpool fans could have been heard in Spain. Easily.

Four goals; the impossible had become a stunning reality. Messi looked baffled, as though he were in the wrong film, and well he might. Who would have believed such a comeback to have been achievable? Perhaps those with memories of Milan in May 2005 in the UEFA Champions League Final in Turkey. 3-0 down, the team had come back within 6 dramatic minutes to score three and then win the match on penalties 3-2.

But the last agonising minutes now had to fall away for the team and the fans. Liverpool, however, were not about to become fainthearted, about to stop fighting; they continued to take the game to Barcelona with more attempts at goal.

And the when the final whistle came, no one had any superlatives left to describe the drama of what had just happened. It was, as one commentator said, a majestic win. Indeed it had been.

With the extraordinary match and victory behind them, it was easy to forget that this had been only the semi-final; it was vital that the team did not repeat Barcelona's failures when they met Tottenham in the final in June in Madrid.

**As history shows, they most certainly did not.**

It mattered not that the goals were less spectacular,

the first coming within just two minutes as Salah put away a penalty.

Liverpool surged forward firing at the Spurs' goal, determined that they would not let the Barca match fade into insignificance and would come away with their first trophy since winning the Football League Cup in 2012. They took every chance to catch the Tottenham keeper off guard with a series of long-range shots, Andrew Robertson's mighty rocket in the 37th minute being one of the most impressive, only cleared with a terrific save from the Spurs keeper.

Tottenham were rarely given the chance to get into threatening positions by the fiery Liverpudlians, who were themselves getting more and more dangerous. But it all came to nothing as the final 15 minutes began to drop away and Tottenham renewed their attacks. Liverpool harried them relentlessly rendering most of their attempts ineffective. With two exceptions; in the 79th minute Alisson performed two magnificent saves within seconds of each other, the second a superb diving clearance in the 84th minute to spare Red blushes. Liverpool seemed to have lost concentration as Tottenham now took the game to them.

MOHAMED SALAH CELEBRATES WITH JORDAN HENDERSON AFTER SCORING THE OPENING GOAL AGAINST TOTTENHAM, JUNE 01, 2019 →

LIVERPOOL CELEBRATE ON AN OPEN-TOP BUS DURING THE UEFA CHAMPIONS LEAGUE VICTORY PARADE, JUNE 2, 2019

Two minutes later a bungled Tottenham defensive mess left Origi clear to put in Liverpool's number two. This was the football of champions, the eye for the half-chance when under pressure, and who but a Tottenham fan would have denied that Liverpool deserved that trophy.

Liverpool had won the UEFA Champions League. An extraordinary finale to a wonderful season of football.

Although it may have seemed like a bad omen, losing to Manchester City in the Community Shield match in August 2019, 5-4 on penalties after a 1-1 draw, the disappointment turned out to be just a minor a hiccup in another superlative season. And the Reds wasted little time in stamping out that loss - and later getting the sweetest revenge on the team that had dealt it.

The first blow in the Liverpool offensive was struck just 10 days later when Liverpool faced Chelsea in the UEFA Super Cup final on August the 14th. When a penalty cancelled out Mané's two goals forcing a penalty shoot out, this time Liverpool pulled the irons out of the fire with a 5-4 win.

**The real drama, however, was happening in the Premier League.**

It had started on the 9th of August with Liverpool dispatching Norwich City 4-1. Fine, expected, as poor Norwich thrashed around at the bottom of the league. What then happened surpassed expectation.

27 games without defeat; in fact, 27 games with just one draw against Manchester United in Manchester, so 26 wins in 27 games. The Reds steamrollered the opposition wherever it came at them - 2-1 against

Chelsea and Tottenham, 3-1 against Manchester City, revenge indeed (in a thrilling match, Fabinho's ferociously low shot from 25 yards out went into the bottom-left corner to put the Reds ahead after six minutes, to be followed by Salah's header seven minutes later, and on 51 minutes, a pinpoint cross from Jordan Henderson found Mane's head and goal number 3), 4-0 against Leicester, 2-0 against Manchester United, the victories poured in until by the time the Covid-19 virus hit the world's consciousness and the league was suspended on the 5th of April 2020, Liverpool were so far ahead as to be almost unreachable (having lost inexplicably in February 3-0 to Watford, 4th from bottom when the season was interrupted, and putting paid to Liverpool's 44 match unbeaten run in the league, which was the second longest in the history of top-flight football). They were 25 points ahead of Manchester City – which must be a revenge record! Also an English top-flight record and surpassing their own 1972 record are the 22 consecutive home wins; and they equalled the Premier League record of 18 consecutive wins.

Not to forget, of course, that by this time Liverpool had already clocked up another first; in December 2019, they had won their first FIFA Club World Cup, defeating Brazilian club Flamengo 1-0 in the final through a Firmino goal on 99 minutes. Mané, running from left to right was played through, delivering a pass to Firmino, charging forwards unmarked, who tapped the ball to his right foot before thundering it past keeper Diego Alves. Liverpool became the first English side to win the international treble of the UEFA Champions League, UEFA Super Cup and FIFA Club World Cup.

There were a few moments of bleakness, of course. One of them came against Chelsea, who knocked Liverpool out of the FA Cup in the 5th round 2-0. Another was the painful defeat in the second leg of the UEFA Champions League match against Atlético Madrid. Liverpool lost both legs, 1-0 in Spain and 2-3 in

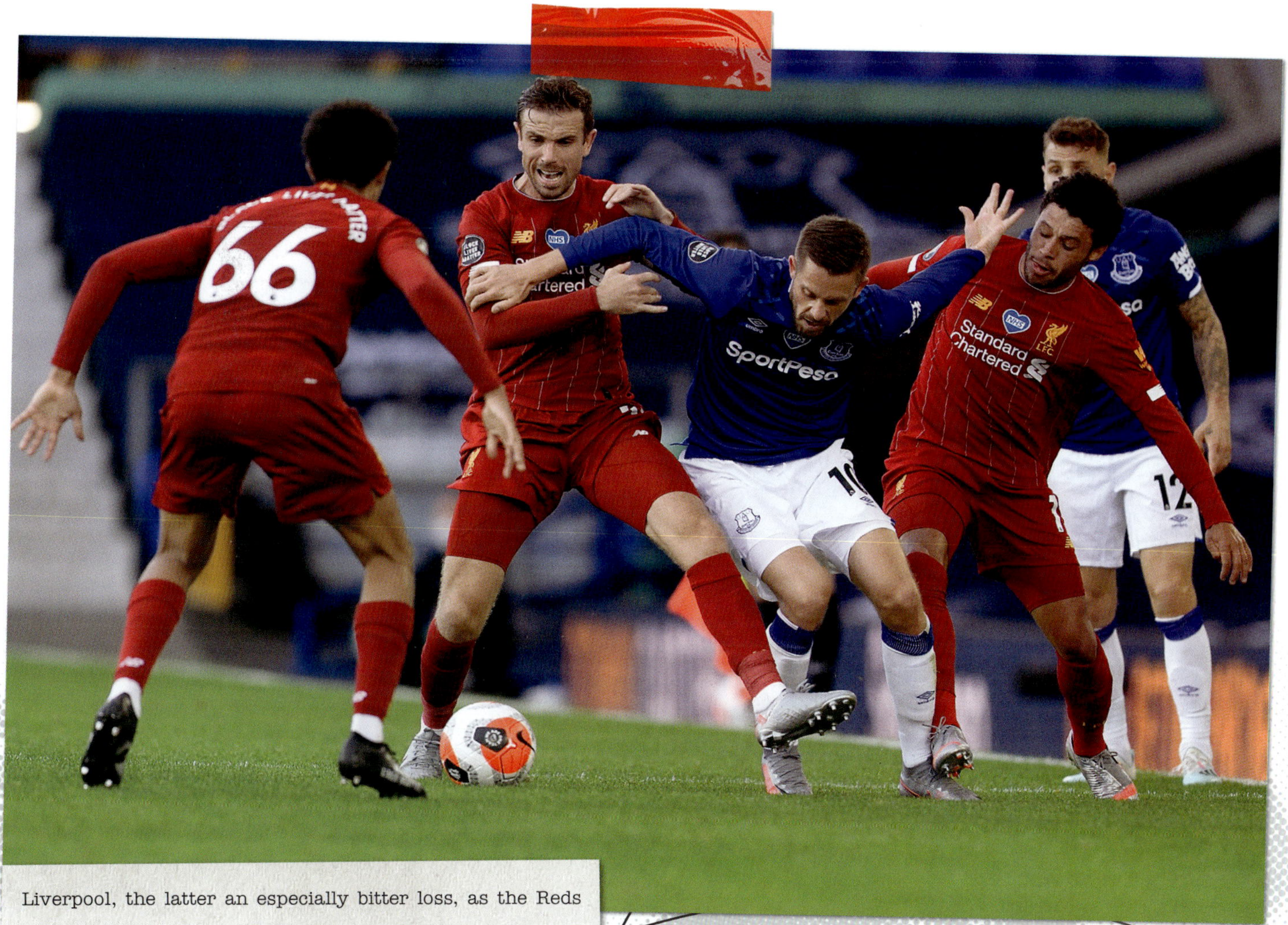

Liverpool, the latter an especially bitter loss, as the Reds had been in charge until extra time. Adrian had made a stupid mistake in such a high stakes match and that had given the Spaniards renewed hope, by playing the ball directly to Joao Felix and slipping before he could save the resulting shot at goal. Water under the bridge.

After 100 days, on the 21st June 2020, the Premier League matches resumed after the Corona virus shutdown, with Liverpool needing just one win to secure the championship. They ran out against Everton, who by then were lounging around in the middle of the table, in Liverpool. Expectations were high, therefore, of clinching the title - but the ecstasy had to be put on hold when all that the Reds brought home was a 0-0 draw. Liverpool held its breath.

LIVERPOOL'S DUTCH MIDFIELDER GEORGINIO WIJNALDUM & ARSENAL'S FRENCH STRIKER ALEXANDRE LACAZETTE 'TAKE A KNEE' IN SUPPORT OF THE BLACK LIVES MATTER MOVEMENT AT THE EMIRATES STADIUM IN LONDON ON JULY 15, 2020

Three days later, at home to Crystal Palace, the Reds shrugged off the months of inactivity and let rip, with Alexander-Arnold, Salah, Fabinho and Mané pounding the visitors' net. Now they were so far ahead in the league that there was a chance for the title to come their way without scoring another goal if Manchester City could be

LIVERPOOL FC CELEBRATING WITH HIS TROPHY OF CHAMPIONS DURING THE FIFA CLUB WORLD CUP FINAL MATCH BETWEEN LIVERPOOL FC AND CR FLAMENGO AT KHALIFA INTERNATIONAL STADIUM ON DECEMBER 21, 2019 IN DOHA, QATAR

SADIO MANE OF LIVERPOOL TAKES A KNEE IN SUPPORT OF THE BLACK LIVES MATTER MOVEMENT PRIOR TO THE PREMIER LEAGUE MATCH BETWEEN LIVERPOOL FC AND CHELSEA FC AT ANFIELD ON JULY 22, 2020

persuaded to fluff their match at Chelsea on June 25th. They could and did, losing 2-1.

The long, long wait of 30 years was finally over. Liverpool were the Premier League champions, champions of England for the 19th time. No team in the history of the Premier League has ever sealed the title at such an early stage. With 86 points to Manchester City's 63, the Reds could no longer be caught even if they stayed on the bench until the end of the season, so great had been their domination of the competition. Despite a 53-day injury to Fabinho and keeper Alisson's 67-day enforced break.

**This was a personal triumph for Jürgen Klopp, now the first German manager to bring an English club to a Premier League title.**

It would be surprising if being crowned so early did not have some effect on the players as they entered the final games of the season and perhaps the 4-0 defeat to a razor-sharp Manchester City at the beginning of July was always going to be on the cards. The Reds recovered some equilibrium to win the next two games against lowly Aston Villa and Brighton but then stumbled again with a 1-1 draw to Burnley at home and a loss to Arsenal 2-1.

So with hopes that the Reds would at least win the difficult match against 3rd-placed Chelsea at home, and then away to Newcastle in the last game of the season, the fans were, in fact, treated to an absolute cracker of a game against Chelsea. Naby Laye Keïta was the first to strike after 23 minutes with a thundering shot from 25 yards, and then the flood gates opened. Alexander-Arnold and then Georginio Wijnaldum causing havoc in the Chelsea defence had made it three for Liverpool before the break, Chelsea just managing to squeeze one in before half-time.

There was more thrilling football to come; Liverpool forged ahead when Firmino struck on the 55th minute and it seemed as though it was all over. But Chelsea fought doggedly on and hit the back of the net twice to make the match an open book at 4-3. Alex Oxlade-Chamberlain was having none of that after the team had played so well. When Liverpool surged forward following a Chelsea free kick, Oxlade-Chamberlain made the final score 5-3.

This was a magnificent way to end the day on which Liverpool were able to celebrate lifting the Premiership title by getting their hands on the cup, now festooned with red ribbons..

It was an emotional day, of course. Over the tannoy, "You'll Never Walk Alone" sounded out and a jubilant Klopp led the singing.

TRENT ALEXANDER-ARNOLD SCORES THE SECOND GOAL FOR LIVERPOOL FC DURING THE MATCH WITH CHELSEA FC AT ANFIELD ON JULY 22, 2020 →

"I was never on The Kop before", he told reporters. "It was pretty special, and I think it makes sense in the moment when the people are not in that we use the Kop to celebrate it with them together in our hearts. It was really good. We are champions of England, Europe and the world", he enthused.

So that left just one final task to end this incredible season. The final game at Newcastle. It was a chance to bask in the sense of achievement; but not to coast home. Mohamed Salah, Sadio Mané and Roberto Firmino were observing from the bench, and could watch in disbelief as the Reds found themselves one down after just 25 seconds.... the fastest goal ever on the final day of a Premier League match. But champions are made of special steel and Liverpool soon put an end to the upstarts with Virgil van Dijk's header levelling the score and a Divock Origi strike from 20 yards putting Liverpool ahead. It only remained for Andrew Robertson's pass to Mané to be curled home for the Reds to end a season of superlatives on a high note, 3-1.

LIVERPOOL CELEBRATE AFTER WINNING THE PREMIER LEAGUE TITLE AT ANFIELD ON JULY 22, 2020. THE STADIUM REMAINED EMPTY DUE TO THE COVID-19 PANDEMIC ↑

The ongoing COVID-19 crowd restrictions and the inevitable hangover from their Premier League triumph were always going to make the 2020-21 season challenging for the Reds. Liverpool were quiet in the summer transfer market, signing midfielder Thiago from Bayern Munich and striker Diogo Jota from Wolves for a combined £61 million, but despite keeping together the core group of players that had made history, Klopp's team could not hit the same heights again.

Three Premier League wins on the bounce to kick-off the new campaign, including victories over both Chelsea and Arsenal, suggested it was business as usual for the defending champions, but a shock 7-2 demolition away at Aston Villa in October was a body blow from which they never fully recovered. Losing key defenders Virgil van Dijk, Joël Matip and Joe Gomez to lengthy injury lay-offs didn't help their cause and by the end of the league season, the Reds had to settle for third and Champions League qualification.

It was a similar story of frustration in the cups. The Reds went out of the League Cup in the fourth round, losing on penalties to Arsenal, while dreams of lifting the FA Cup were ended in January after a thrilling but painful 3-2 defeat against Man United at Old Trafford.

European glory and another Champions League success became the side's focus. Liverpool cruised through the early stages as Group D winners and were ruthless in knocking out RB Leipzig 4-0 on aggregate in the Last 16. Spanish giants Real Madrid stood in their way in the quarter-finals and a 3-1 defeat at the Bernabéu in the first leg, which was followed by a goalless draw at Anfield eight days later, decided the tie.

If anyone however believed that the Reds had reached their peak under Klopp after a season, his fifth in charge, without silverware were wrong. The 2021-22 campaign was one which saw Liverpool come roaring back in spectacular style and although they agonisingly missed out on an unprecedented quadruple, the Anfield faithful were not complaining after watching two more trophies added to the club's collection.

The battle for the Premier League title with Man City was monumental and only decided on the final day of the season. The Reds were beaten only twice in the league all year - losing on the road to West Ham and Leicester - but City were equally dominant and as the two rivals lined up for their respective 38th and final league fixtures, the Manchester club were just one point ahead of Klopp's side. Liverpool did their job, beating Wolves 3-1 at Anfield thanks to goals from Sadio Mané, Mo Salah and Andy Robertson to keep up the pressure on City, but Pep Guardiola's side didn't blink, coming back from 2-1 down against Aston Villa at the Etihad with two crucial late scores to wrap up a 3-2 win and the Premier League trophy.

It was heartbreaking but the Reds had already enjoyed a pair of famous victories in 2022 that helped ease the pain. Klopp had not won either the League or FA Cup since arriving on Merseyside in late 2015, but he added both to his CV as Liverpool enjoyed two triumphant trips to Wembley.

Their march to the League Cup final began with comfortable wins over Norwich and Preston before they needed penalties to despatch Leicester in the last eight. Unsurprisingly the semi-final against Arsenal was another tough test, especially after the first leg at Anfield finished goalless, but a double from Diogo Jota in the return game was enough to book the Reds a place in a Wembley showpiece game for the first time in six years.

DIOGO JOTA SCORES HIS SECOND GOAL FOR LIVERPOOL AGAINST ARSENAL IN THE LEAGUE CUP SEMI-FINAL SECOND LEG, JANUARY 20, 2022

KEEPER SPOT KICK HEROICS FROM CAOIMHIN KELLEHER IN THE LEAGUE CUP FINAL, AS HE SCORES FOR LIVERPOOL, FEBRUARY 27, 2022

Chelsea stood in their way and after 90 minutes and extra time in north London, there were no goals. Remarkably the shootout that followed saw both sides on target with their first 10 penalties apiece and with every outfield player in red and blue having stepped forward, it was the goalkeepers' turn to try their luck. Reds stopper Caoimhín Kelleher was the first to nervously place the ball on the spot and was a picture of joy and relief as he netted into the top corner. Back between the sticks Kelleher then watched as his opposite number, Kepa Arrizabalaga, blasted over the bar.

The dramatic win at Wembley gave Liverpool their ninth victory in the League Cup, making the Reds the most successful club in the history of the competition.

ALISSON COMES TO THE RESCUE FOR LIVERPOOL IN THE FA CUP FINAL, MAKING A CRUCIAL SAVE IN THE PENALTY SHOOTOUT, MAY 14, 2022

Less than three months later Klopp's team were back at the home of football for the FA Cup final in May and Chelsea were again the opponents. Liverpool had knocked out Man City in the semi-final, beating their rivals 3-2 in Manchester, but there was no repeat of that free-flowing football in the final as both sides cancelled each other out. Luis Díaz and Andy Robertson both hit the woodwork at Wembley but there was ultimately nothing to separate the sides after 120 minutes of play and another shootout loomed.

This time it was Alisson and not Kelleher wearing the gloves for the Reds, but the result was the same. James Milner, Thiago, Firmino and Trent Alexander-Arnold were all on target for Liverpool and although Sadio Mané's effort was saved, Alisson levelled things up at 5-5 when he denied Mason Mount. Greek defender Kostas Tsimikas

THE WIDE SMILE SAYS IT ALL FOR KLOPP, AS HE JOYOUSLY HOLDS UP THE FA CUP AFTER LIVERPOOL DEFEATED CHELSEA FOR THE SECOND TIME AT WEMBLEY IN 2022

was the man with the chance to give the Reds victory and he made no mistake when it mattered, calmly sending Blues keeper Édouard Mendy the wrong way.

For the eighth time Liverpool had lifted the FA Cup. The win was the first time in 16 years the Reds had triumphed in the game's oldest cup competition and completed Klopp's personal clean sweep of the three major English football honours. It was also the second time the Reds had sealed the domestic cup double, following the team's heroics under Gérard Houllier 21 years earlier, making Liverpool the only club in history to twice claim the FA and League Cup in the same season.

Two cups almost became three as Klopp's side came agonisingly close to winning the Champions League in 2022. Drawn in what looked like the group of death alongside Atlético Madrid, Porto and AC Milan, they stormed into the knockout stages with six wins from six. The Reds then easily eliminated Inter Milan, Benfica and Villarreal to book their place in the final and a clash with 13-time champions Real Madrid in Paris.

A repeat of the 2018 final, which Madrid had won 3-1, the rematch was a one-sided game where Liverpool dominated but still somehow lost. The Reds had a total of 24 shots, nine on target, compared to Real's meagre four. Mo Salah saw six efforts saved by Thibaut Courtois, who also deflected a Sadio Mané attempt onto the post, while the only goal of the game came in the 59th minute when Vinícius Júnior beat Alisson from close range.

THE REDS POSE BEFORE THEIR CHAMPIONS LEAGUE FINAL WITH MADRID AT THE STADE DE FRANCE, MAY 28, 2022

KLOPP WAS CERTAINLY MAKING HIS MARK AS A LIVERPOOL MANAGER TO BE RECKONED WITH

FACING CHELSEA ONCE AGAIN IN A LEAGUE CUP FINAL, VIRGIL VAN DIJK SCORES IN EXTRA TIME FOR LIVERPOOL TO SECURE VICTORY, FEBRUARY 25, 2024

HONOURARY SCOUSER – KLOPP THANKS THE ANFIELD FAITHFUL, MAY 19, 2024

With two more trophies in the bag, hopes were high ahead of 2022-23 but Liverpool's challenge for more silverware faltered. They were off the pace in the league from the start, finally finishing fifth, while their displays in knockout football failed to reproduce the previous season's magic. Fourth round exits in both the FA and League Cup meant the Champions League was the Reds' only remaining chance of success but yet again their nemesis, Real Madrid, put an end to their European adventure after decisively overcoming Klopp's side 6-2 on aggregate in the Last 16.

The 2023-24 campaign was to be Klopp's ninth and final year in the hot seat. His contract ran until 2026 but in a move that stunned the Anfield faithful, the club revealed in January the German would be leaving at the end of the season. Klopp admitted he was simply out of gas and the time had come to make way for a new manager.

It was shock news but with four trophies still on offer when the Reds confirmed Klopp's impending exit, there was work to be done. Only two days before the announcement, the team had booked their place in the League Cup final and in February they travelled down to Wembley to face Chelsea. It was another close affair against the Blues, but this time there was no need of a penalty shootout after a Van Dijk header two minutes before the end of extra time sealed victory.

The seventh major title of his Liverpool reign ensured Klopp would leave Merseyside in style. The Reds would dearly have loved to make it eight trophies for the popular German but had to settle for their Wembley triumph and gave the manager a predictably emotional but uplifting send-off at Anfield in his final ever fixture, a 2-0 win over Wolves in May. It was his 491st game at the helm and the end of one of the most successful and entertaining eras in the club's history.

19
YOU'LL NEVER WALK ALONE
LIVERPOOL
FOOTBALL CLUB
EST 1892
LIVERPOOL FC
v Wolverhampton Wanderers FC
19/05/2024 • Kick-off 4pm
OFFICIAL LIVERPOOL FC MATCHDAY PROGRAMME
DANKE JÜRGEN
Match Sponsor
standard chartered
AXA
Expedia

# SLOTTING RIGHT IN

Even as the applause rang out at Anfield in May to bid goodbye to Klopp, Liverpool fans already knew who had been chosen to fill the German's sizeable shoes. The official confirmation that Arne Slot would be the club's new manager came the day after the end of the season but news that the Dutchman was on his way to Merseyside had been an open secret for weeks.

The 45-year-old was a fascinating appointment. One of a new generation of young, exciting European coaches, Slot already had eight years of touchline experience under his belt but had neither played nor managed outside the Netherlands before. Winning the Dutch league title in 2023, as well as lifting the Cup a year later, during his three seasons at the helm of Feyenoord was proof Slot had the ability to secure silverware, but swapping the Eredivisie for the bright lights of the Premier League was still a significant step up in terms of quality and expectations.

Klopp's legacy was a strong one. The spine of the team that had reached the final of the Champions League only two years earlier was still largely intact. Centre-back Joël Matip and midfielder Thiago were the only senior players to leave Anfield in the summer that Slot arrived and although there were no eye-catching signings in the transfer window, the new manager inherited a squad with experience, firepower and a proven track record for success.

The eagerly anticipated Slot era began with a pre-season tour to the United States. A 3-0 victory over old rivals Manchester United in Columbia in early August inevitably endeared him to the Liverpool faithful but the real challenges still lay ahead, the first being the Premier League opener at Ipswich two weeks later. Second-half goals from Diogo Jota and Mohamed Salah sealed a 2-0 win at Portman Road and three points and although it was a workmanlike rather than pyrotechnic display, Slot was up and running. Curiously the Dutchman was the first permanent Liverpool manager in sole charge to win his opening league fixture since Graeme Souness as far back as 1991.

Anfield had the chance to welcome their new

TAKING OVER FROM KLOPP WAS A TALL ORDER TO SAY THE LEAST, BUT SLOT TOOK THE CHALLENGE IN HIS STRIDE

man properly eight days later when the Reds hosted Brentford. Slot's energetic side delivered a 2-0 victory thanks to Luis Díaz and Salah and if the fans were already warming to their Dutch coach, they fell in love with him after his team completely dismantled Manchester United at Old Trafford. The 3-0 scoreline didn't do justice to Liverpool's dominance and after three games, three wins and three clean sheets; Slot had already underlined his credentials.

A GREAT START FOR LIVERPOOL AT PORTMAN ROAD. DIOGO JOTA SCORES THE FIRST GOAL FOR THE REDS AND HIS MANAGERS MAIDEN GAME AT IPSWICH, AUGUST 17, 2024

A shock 1-0 defeat to Nottingham Forest at Anfield next time out proved to be only a temporary setback. The Reds would not taste defeat at home for the remainder of their Premier League campaign and as the season unfolded, it became increasingly evident Slot had hit on a winning formula. At times his team were more pragmatic than they had been under Klopp but the attacking threat remained and the results followed.

After their Forest upset, the Reds went 26 league games unbeaten. They went top in early November after beating Brighton 2-1 on Merseyside courtesy of second-half goals from Cody Gakpo and Salah and as the superb

IN THEIR MATCH AT ANFIELD, LIVERPOOL'S JOE GOMEZ HEADS THE BALL TOWARDS THE GOAL OF BRIGHTON, NOVEMBER 2, 2024

sequence continued, belief that Slot could bring home the title in his debut season grew. Highlights of their undefeated run included home and away victories over reigning champions Manchester City, both 2-0 wins, a 6-3 drubbing of Tottenham in north London and another comprehensive win in the capital, the 5-0 crushing of West Ham in their final fixture of 2024.

London however was finally the team's undoing when they were ambushed 3-2 by Fulham at Craven Cottage in early April. The end of the magnificent run was unexpected but when the final whistle sounded at Fulham, the Reds still enjoyed an 11-point lead in the table over second-place Arsenal and with just seven games left - from which Slot's side needed four victories to become champions - their destiny was firmly in their own hands.

They ultimately only needed three more games for glory. Wins over West Ham and Leicester quickly banished memories of the result against the Cottagers

LIVERPOOL FANS CELEBRATE WHAT HAS BEEN A TREMENDOUS FIRST YEAR FOR ARNE SLOT. IF THERE WAS ANY GAMBLE IN HIS APPOINTMENT, THEN IT CERTAINLY PAID OFF

# CHAMP 20NS

A CHEEKY SELFIE FOR SALAH, AS HE TAKES GOAL CELEBRATIONS TO THE NEXT LEVEL AFTER SCORING LIVERPOOL'S FOURTH GOAL AGAINST TOTTENHAM AT ANFIELD, APRIL 27, 2025

and at the same time the Gunners' challenge faltered. It meant that the team needed only a point from their clash with Spurs at Anfield in late April to wrap up the title and give Slot a fairy-tale first season with the club.

There was a party atmosphere on Merseyside ahead of the game but the celebrations were briefly put on hold when Dominic Solanke, a former Red, gave Spurs a 12th-minute lead but just four minutes later Díaz settled any lingering nerves with the equaliser. Alexis Mac Allister put Liverpool in front midway through the first half and after Gakpo made it 3-1 before half-time, the result was never again in doubt. Unsurprisingly it was Salah who added a fourth after the break before an own goal concluded the scoring and the Reds were 5-1 winners.

The scenes at Anfield after the final whistle were unforgettable. Denied the chance to celebrate with their fans after winning the title in 2020 due to Covid restrictions, the team and their victorious manager made the most of the moment. The fact their triumph had also equalled Manchester United's record of 20 top-flight crowns was the icing on the cake. As Anfield rocked, Slot paid tribute to his players and his predecessor.

"They always find a way to win," he said. "I'm incredibly proud, not only of the players but the people standing here, sport directors, my staff members, we should give them a big round of applause. Let's forget it's the second title in 35 years, it's the second in five years. When the season started, we would have been happy with top four. But I don't think that is fair on the players as they are much better than that and they have shown it this season.

"It feels great. The only thing now is to send my appreciation to Jürgen Klopp. I am 99.9% sure that if I pick up my phone there will be a message from Jürgen. So many moments in the season the two of us have had contact. I think he showed last season what a wonderful human being he is by introducing me. But what mattered most is the team he left behind that was able to win the trophy."

The story of Liverpool's challenges in cup competition in 2024-25 was a mixed one. They were stunned by Championship side Plymouth Argyle in the fourth round of the FA Cup, losing 1-0 at Home Park, but the Champions League promised much more. The Reds finished top of the revamped 36-team group stage of the competition, winning seven of their games en route to the Last 16 and a showdown with Paris Saint-Germain. It needed a penalty shootout at Anfield to separate the two teams, which Slot's side heartbreakingly lost, but the result was put into context two months later when the French side were crowned the champions of Europe.

In the League Cup the Reds came agonisingly close to making it a trophy double in Slot's debut season. The draw was not kind to them with Premier League opposition in every round of the competition but each time the team rose to the challenge, despatching West Ham, Brighton and Southampton before recovering from a 1-0 loss to Spurs in London in the first leg of their semi-final with an irresistible 4-0 victory in the return fixture at Anfield.

For the fifth time they faced top-flight rivals in the final in the shape of Newcastle United. The two earlier Premier League meetings with the Magpies had ended with a dramatic 3-3 draw at St James' Park in December followed by a 2-0 win for Slot's side in February at Anfield, but less than three weeks after the match on

TAKING CENTRE STAGE, SLOT TAKES IN THE MAGNIFICENT ACHIEVEMENT OF LIVERPOOL AGAIN BECOMING PREMIER LEAGUE CHAMPIONS, MAY 25, 2025

GETTING THE PARTY STARTED, THE REDS TOOK TO THE STREETS OF LIVERPOOL IN OPEN-TOP BUSES TO THE DELIGHT OF THE HUGE MERSEYSIDE CROWDS

Merseyside, Newcastle turned the tables at Wembley.

Goals shortly before and after half-time gave United a 2-0 lead and although summer signing Federico Chiesa came off the bench to reduce the arrears in injury time with his second goal for the club, it was too little too late to change the outcome. The Magpies lifted the trophy and Liverpool were denied.

On balance the result at Wembley was a disappointment rather than disaster. The Reds' faithful did not have long to wait for the team's coronation as Premier League champions and there was no question which silverware both Slot and the fans would have chosen at the start of the season in which no one was sure what could be achieved after Klopp's glorious reign. The new manager had laid down a marker in the most convincing style possible and as the summer arrived, the squad and supporters alike were already dreaming, with good reason, of a 21st league title and a standalone place in English football's record books.

# THE PLAYERS

THIS IS A SHORT GUIDE TO SOME OF THE GREATEST LIVERPOOL PLAYERS, ALTHOUGH THE SUPPORTERS OF ONE PLAYER OR ANOTHER WILL ALWAYS DISPUTE SUCH A LIST. BUT HERE ARE THE NAMES OF SOME OF THOSE WHO MUST ALWAYS APPEAR

## KENNY DALGLISH

Kenneth Dalglish was born on the 4th March 1951. In a career that lasted 22 years he won the Balloon d'Or Silver Award as well as PFA Player of the Year In 1983. He received the FWA Footballer of the Year in 1979 and 1983 and in 2009, FourFourTwo named him as the greatest striker in post-war football in Britain. In 2006 he came top of the Liverpool fans' "100 Players Who Shook the Kop" poll and he has been inducted into both the English and Scottish Football Halls of Fame.

" . . . Dalglish wants to get on but I would have moved heaven and earth to keep him. I would rather have quit and got out of the game altogether than sold a player of his brilliance." These were Bill Shankly's words when he heard that Dalglish was coming to Liverpool and showed the esteem in which Dalglish was held in the football world.

Dalglish played his first match for Liverpool on the 13th August 1977 in a 0-0 draw against Man United. His first League goal came one week later against Middlesbrough and he finished the first season at Liverpool with 31 goals to his credit and had also scored the winning goal against Bruges in the 1978 European Cup final.

The following season he was named Football Writers Association Footballer of the Year.

Dalglish became manager of Liverpool when Joe Fagan retired in 1985 to become the first player manager in English football. He became one of Liverpool's most successful managers and as a player scored the winning goal against Chelsea to give Liverpool their 16th League title.

He made 515 appearances for Liverpool playing his last match on the 1st May 1990 having scored 172 goals for the club.

# IAN RUSH

Born on the 20th November 1961 in Wales he made his Liverpool debut on the 13th December 1980 in a 1-1 draw against Ipswich Town.

Ian Rush was one of the top strikers in English football during the 1980s and 1990s and made 73 appearances for the Welsh national football team where he remains top goalscorer with 28 goals. He also remains top goalscorer for Liverpool scoring 346 goals in all competitions for the Reds.

He has been voted PFA Young Player of the Year, PFA Players' Player of the Year and FWA Footballer of the Year 5 times; he was awarded the European Golden Boot in 1984 and the First Division Golden Boot the same year. He was Liverpool's top goalscorer over nine seasons. He also holds the record for the most FA Cup final goals scored, having five to his credit and is the second top FA Cup scorer of all time, the highest in the 20th century with 44 goals.

After a slow build up, Rush scored his first goal on 30 September 1981 in a European Cup tie with his first League goals coming less than two weeks later, on the 10th October 1981 when Liverpool beat Leeds United 3-0. After that, Rush became an unstoppable goalscorer and put the ball into the net 30 times in 49 appearances in all competitions in the 1981/82 season.

Rush accepted an offer to leave Liverpool for Juventus on the 22nd July 1986.

He returned to Anfield after one season in Italy and stayed until 1996. In the 1989-90 season Rush won his fifth and final League title with Liverpool finishing nine points clear. In 1995 he gained his 5th League Cup winners' medal. He played his last game at Anfield on 27 April 1997. He was voted The Writers Association Footballer of the Year.

## KEVIN KEEGAN

Born on the 14th February 1951 he made his debut for Liverpool on the 14th August 1971 in a 3-1 victory over Nottingham Forest when he scored after 12 minutes.

"I was just as sure of Keegan as I was of Denis Law and I never had cause to think again about Denis. These two players are so much alike in a number of ways. Keegan is an exciting boy all right," said Bill Shankly in 1971.

Keegan became a football superstar in the 1970s and 1980s. He won three First Division titles at Liverpool, one FA Cup, one European Cup and two UEFA Cups. He became European Footballer of the Year in 1978 and 1979. He was capped for England 63 times and scored 21 goals.

The 1974/75 season was perhaps the lowest point of his career when he was sent off after a scuffle with Billy Bremner of Leeds receiving a lengthy ban.

Keegan scored 100 goals in his 323 appearances for the Reds.

Keegan was one of the most talented and enthusiastic players at the club, who was generous in his playing making great chances for his colleagues with intelligent passes and is remembered as one of the finest players to run out onto the Anfield pitch.

## RAY CLEMENCE

Born on the 5th August 1948 he made his Liverpool debut on the 25th September 1968. He appeared for the club 665 times and became one of the most decorated goalkeepers in English and European football and was considered to be one of Liverpool's greatest, if not the greatest goalkeeper.

Bill Shankly nurtured his young goalkeeper in the reserve side for another two years and Clemence became first-team permanent goalkeeper in 1970. His most famous save was perhaps in the UEFA cup against Borussia Mönchengladbach when he saved a penalty and Liverpool won 3-2 on aggregate.

With Liverpool he won the Football League First Division title five times, the FA Cup and the League Cup once and the UEFA Cup twice, the European Cup three times and the UEFA Super Cup once. He was awarded an MBE for services to football.

"Ray was one of the best goalkeepers I have ever seen" said Ian Callaghan. "He is in England's top three alongside Gordon Banks and Peter Shilton. No one dominated the box as well as Clem. He made things look easy which is the sign of a top keeper."

## EMLYN HUGHES

Born on the 28th August 1947 he died on the 9th November 2004 from a brain tumor. He made his Liverpool debut on the 4th March 1967 and appeared for Liverpool in 665 games earning himself the nickname "Crazy Horse". He became the first captain of the Reds to win the European Cup in 1977 the same year as he was named FWA Footballer of the Year. With Liverpool he won the Football League First Division four times, the FA Cup once, the European Cup twice, the UEFA Cup twice and the UEFA Super Cup once.

Hughes and Phil Thompson formed a creative partnership setting up Liverpool's attacks from behind with midfield passes instead of lofting the ball up the field. Hughes was not the best loved of players on the field and Bob Paisley thought that he might have been an even better player but for his personality.

Hughes played for the club for twelve and a half years.

## IAN CALLAGHAN

Born on the 10th April 1942 he played his first match for Liverpool on the 16th April 1960 and appeared for the club in a record-breaking 857 games.

He joined the club as an apprentice on the 28th March 1960 and was a regular in the team from 1961 onwards and also played for England where he was a member of the World Cup-winning team in 1966. He was FWA footballer of the year in 1974 and was awarded the MBE the same year. He spent 18 years with the club and won the League title five times, the FA Cup twice, the European Cup twice, the UEFA Cup twice and the UEFA Super Cup once.

Callaghan was only booked once in his career and never sent off the field. He was the quintessential team player.

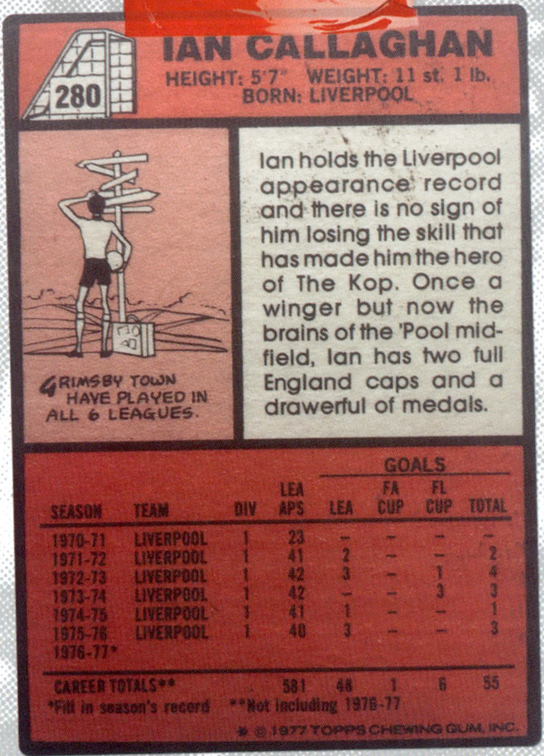

**IAN CALLAGHAN**

280

HEIGHT: 5'7" WEIGHT: 11 st. 1 lb.
BORN: LIVERPOOL

GRIMSBY TOWN HAVE PLAYED IN ALL 6 LEAGUES.

Ian holds the Liverpool appearance record and there is no sign of him losing the skill that has made him the hero of The Kop. Once a winger but now the brains of the 'Pool mid-field, Ian has two full England caps and a drawerful of medals.

| SEASON | TEAM | DIV | LEA APS | GOALS LEA | GOALS FA CUP | GOALS FL CUP | GOALS TOTAL |
|---|---|---|---|---|---|---|---|
| 1970-71 | LIVERPOOL | 1 | 23 | – | – | – | – |
| 1971-72 | LIVERPOOL | 1 | 41 | 2 | – | – | 2 |
| 1972-73 | LIVERPOOL | 1 | 42 | 3 | – | 1 | 4 |
| 1973-74 | LIVERPOOL | 1 | 42 | – | – | 3 | 3 |
| 1974-75 | LIVERPOOL | 1 | 41 | 1 | – | – | 1 |
| 1975-76 | LIVERPOOL | 1 | 40 | 3 | – | – | 3 |
| 1976-77* | | | | | | | |
| CAREER TOTALS** | | | 581 | 48 | 1 | 6 | 55 |

*Fill in season's record **Not including 1976-77

© 1977 TOPPS CHEWING GUM, INC.

## JOHN BARNES

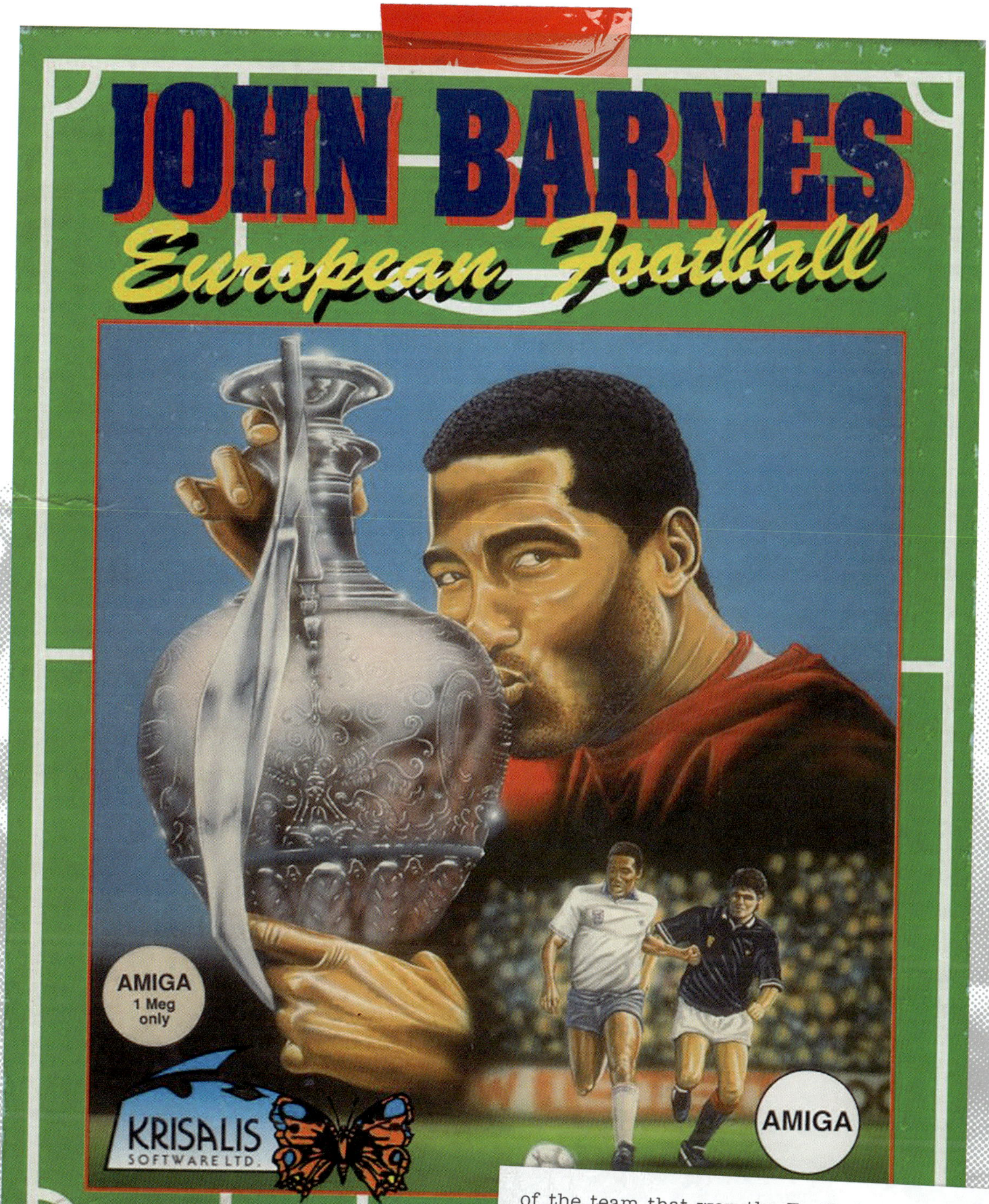


Born on the 7th November 1963 he made his Liverpool debut on the 15th August 1987 against Arsenal. He scored his first goal against Oxford United on the 12th September when Liverpool won 2-1. He made 407 appearances for Liverpool scoring 108 goals and was regarded as one of his club's and the country's best players. With Liverpool he won the Football League First Division twice, the FA Cup twice, and the League Cup and Charity Shield once. He was a member of the team that won the Football League First Division PFA Team of the Year three times, was voted PFA Players Player of the Year in 1988 and was voted FWA Footballer of the Year in 1988 and 1990. He became an MBE in 1998 and was inducted into the English Football Hall of Fame in 2005. On the 6th September 1995 Barnes won his 79th and last international cap for England. Barnes was an extremely talented and graceful player who played exciting fast moving football.

## BILLY LIDDELL

Born on the 10th January 1922 he died on the 3rd July 2001. He made his debut for Liverpool on the 5th January 1946 appearing 534 times for the club, scoring 228 goals. Liddell was essentially a left-winger and was noted for his good professional behaviour, his powerful shooting, his speed and his strength. For the Liverpool supporters of that era he is simply the best player ever to run out in a red shirt. He won the English First Division title, in 1947.

"Liddell was some player" remarked Bill Shankly, "He had everything. He was fast, powerful, shot with either foot and his headers were like blasts from a gun. On top of all that he was as hard as granite. What a player! He was so strong!" Liddell retired at 39 before the Shankly years got under way.

Donald Mackinlay, Liverpool's captain from the 1920's, said of him, "Liverpool have had some good club players, but I think he is the finest in their history."

## ALAN HANSEN

Hansen was born on the 13th June 1955 in Clackmannanshire Scotland.

He made his Liverpool debut on the 24th September 1957 and appeared for the Reds in 620 games scoring 14 goals. Bob Paisley said of him "Alan Hansen . . . is quite simply the most skilful centre-half I have ever seen in the British game and is a joy to watch . . . A player who carries the ball with control and grace." One aspect of his game was that he would dribble the ball away from defence instead of kicking it up field, which caused Paisley to remark "He has given me more heart attacks than any player I have known."

With Liverpool, Hansen won the Football League First Division eight times, the FA Cup twice, the League Cup three times, the FA Charity Shield six times, the European cup three times and the Screen Sports Super Cup once. He also won 26 caps for Scotland.

Hanson was considered to be of the best footballers of his generation and one of the best defenders in the English league.

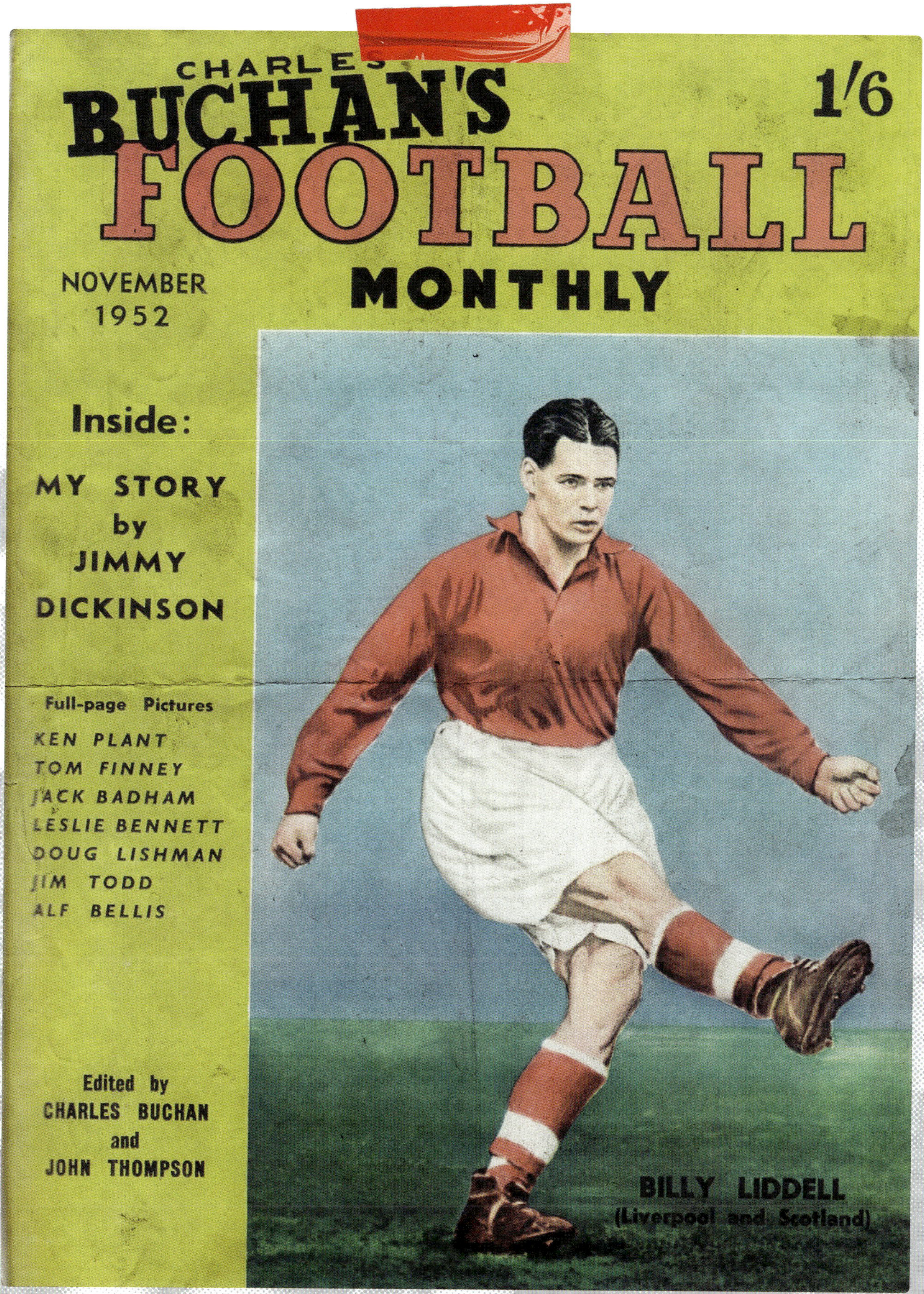
CHARLES
BUCHAN'S
FOOTBALL
MONTHLY
1/6
NOVEMBER
1952
Inside:
MY STORY
by
JIMMY
DICKINSON
Full-page Pictures
KEN PLANT
TOM FINNEY
JACK BADHAM
LESLIE BENNETT
DOUG LISHMAN
JIM TODD
ALF BELLIS
Edited by
CHARLES BUCHAN
and
JOHN THOMPSON
BILLY LIDDELL
(Liverpool and Scotland)

# ‘I’m a Scouser fron never want to lose that’

## STEVEN GERRARD

Steven George Gerrard, MBE was born on the 30th of May 1980 in Whiston, Merseyside.

It was while playing for the Whiston team that he was spotted by Liverpool scouts, joining the Liverpool Academy at just nine years old.

The 6ft (1.83m) midfielder’s debut for the club came on the 29th November 1998 against Blackburn Rovers, and as his talents rapidly matured, he made his debut for the England squad in 2000 and became Liverpool captain in October 2003.

By the time that he left Liverpool to go to LA Galaxy, 17 seasons later in 2015, the man who Zinedine Zidane and Pelé considered to be the best footballer in the world had scored 120 goals for the Reds in 504 appearances in which he helped the team to cup glory in Britain and Europe.

Married to Alex Curran on the 16th of June 2007, Gerrard’s was an extraordinary talent. His passing ability, his tackling skills, his invaluable ability to inspire confidence in those playing around him marked him out as one of the greatest footballers of his age. If there is one game that has to be eternally linked to his name, it is the match against Milan in May 2005 in the UEFA Champion’s League Final in Turkey. 3-0 down, the team came back to win the match with Gerrard in on the goal tally as well. Gerrard spoke from the heart when he said of the game known as the “miracle of Istanbul”, “Lifting the cup as Liverpool captain was just the best moment of my life.”

### HE HAS RECEIVED TWENTY-SEVEN PERSONAL AWARDS, MANY OF THOSE HE RECEIVED ON MULTIPLE OCCASIONS. AMONGST THEM ARE:

- The PFA Young Player of the Year in 2001.
- The Ballon d’Or Bronze Award for 2005 and the UEFA Club Footballer of the Year for 2005.
- The FIFA Club World Championship Silver Ball in 2005.
- The UEFA Champions League Final Man of the Match in 2005.
- The PFA Players’ Player of the Year in 2006.
- The FWA Footballer of the Year in 2009.
- The PFA Fans’ Player of the Year in 2001 and 2009.
- The England Player of the Year Award in 2007 and 2012.
- The Liverpool Player of the Season in 2004, 06, 07 and 09.
- The BBC Goal of the Season in 2006.
- The FA Cup Final Man of the Match in 2006
- The Premier League Player of the Month for March 2001, March 2003, December 2004, April 2006, March 2009 and March 2014.
- The IFFHS World’s Most Popular Footballer in 2006.

a council estate... I

# MICHAEL OWEN

Michael Owen was born on the 14th of December 1979 in Chester, England. He was the fourth child and began playing football when he was seven and was soon playing in the local area Under-11 team becoming captain and smashing a goal-scoring record with 97 goals in one season.

He decided to sign for Liverpool and also played for the England U-15/16 teams and became a professional with Liverpool in 1996 when he was seventeen.

His goal scoring abilities became the stuff of legend and from the start of the 1997/98 season until the 2003/04 season when he left the club for real Madrid, the striker was Liverpool's top goalscorer in consecutive years. His tally was 118 goals in 2016 appearances. He was also capped for England 88 times.

His speed and technical mastery and eye for an opportunity made Owen one of the Premier League's top strikers of all time. Unfortunately, he was bedevilled with injuries which prevented him from carving out an even more illustrious career.

Owen met Louise Bonsall at primary school in 1984 and they married on the 24th of June 2005 and they have three daughters; Gemma Rose, Emily May and Jessica, and one son, Michael.

## AMONGST OTHER AWARDS, OWEN HAS THESE PERSONAL HONOURS:

- The Ballon d'Or in 2001.
- The World Soccer World Player of the Year in 2001.
- The ESM Team of the Year for 2000/01.
- The BBC Sports Personality of the Year in 1998.
- The Premier League Golden Boot for 1997/98 and 1998/99.
- The Premier League Player of the Season in 1997/98.
- The PFA Young Player of the Year for 1997/98.
- The PFA Team of the Year in 1997/98.
- The Premier League Player of the Month in August 1998.
- The FIFA World Cup Best Young Player Award in 1998.
- English Football Hall of Fame: 2014.
- Golden Foot 2017.

OWEN
10
10
9

# MOHAMED SALAH HAMED MAHROUS GHALY

Mohamed Salah, nicknamed 'The Pharaoh', was born in Egypt in 1992. After playing youth football with Al Mokawloon in North Africa, Salah's talent was soon spotted by Swiss team Basel, the team for whom he signed in 2012 on a four-year contract, helping the team win the Swiss Super League season of 2012-13 and the Swiss Cup the following season.

In 2014 he signed for Chelsea, the first Egyptian to play for the club. It was not the happiest of times under manager Jose Mourinho and he was loaned out to Fiorentina for 18 months and he eventually signed for Roma on a loan basis. Less than a year later, he was on his way to Liverpool for a club record fee of £36.5 million. Blessed with speed, dribbling skills, agility and an eye for an opportunity, Salah has proved to be a world-class finisher as well as brilliant creator of chances for team-mates.

Since arriving at Anfield in 2017, the Egyptian has won two Premier League titles, the Champions League, the FIFA Club World Cup, as well as the FA and League Cup. Remarkably he has finished as the club's top scorer in every one of his eight seasons on Merseyside and his haul of 34 goals in 52 appearances in 2024-25 as the Reds romped to the title saw Salah rise to third place in Liverpool's all-time list of goalscorers behind Ian Rush and Roger Hunt.

He netted 29 times in the Premier League in 2024-25 to win the Golden Boot and become only the second player after Thierry Henry to claim the award for a record fourth time.

## SALAH HAS REAPED A HOST OF AWARDS. AMONGST HIS PERSONAL HONOURS ARE:

- CAF Most Promising Talent of the Year 2012.
- UEFA Golden Boy 2012
- SAFP Golden Player 2013.
- AS Roma Player of the Season 2015-16
- Premier League Player of the Month, Nov 2017, Feb 2018, Mar 2018, Oct 2021, Oct 2023, Nov 2024, Feb 2025
- African Footballer of the Year in 2017, 2018
- PFA Player's Player of the Year 2017-18, 2021-22
- FWA Footballer of the Year 2017-18, 2021-22, 2024-25
- Premier League Golden Boot 2017-18, 2018-19, 2021-22, 2024-25
- Premier League Player of the Season 2017-18, 2024-25
- Liverpool Player of the Year 2017-18, 2020-21, 2021-22, 2023-24, 2024-25
- FIFA Club World Cup Golden Ball 2019
- PFA Premier League Team of the Year 2017-18, 2020-21, 2021-22
- Liverpool Goal of the Season 2018-19, 2021-22, 2022-23

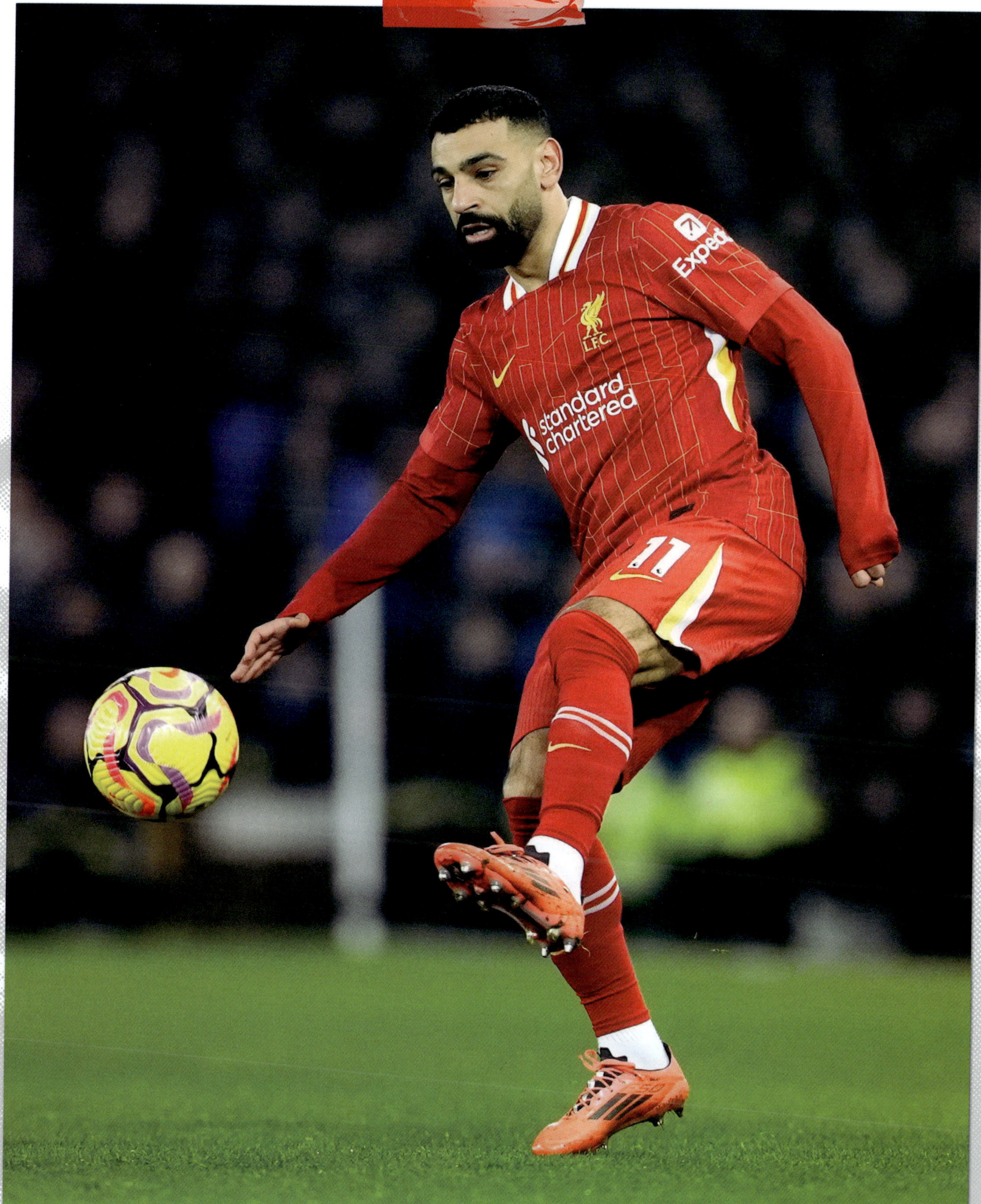
Expedia
standard chartered
LFC
11

# JORDAN HENDERSON

Jordan Henderson was born on the 17th of June 1990 in Sunderland. At the age of 8 years, he was signed up by Sunderland and the midfielder made his first-team debut in November 2008. After three seasons with his hometown club, he joined Liverpool in 2011 after taking the captain's armband in 2015, he was a key member of the side that won the UEFA Champions League, the UEFA Super Cup, the FIFA Club World Cup in 2019 and the Premier League in 2020.

An international since 2010, he became the first English man to win both the England Under-21 and Senior Player of the Year awards. A fierce competitor and natural leader, he won his 50th cap for the Three Lions in 2019 and has played in six major tournaments for his country, featuring in the 2020 European Championship final against Italy. He left Liverpool in 2023 after 12 seasons at Anfield, signing for Saudi Arabian side Al-Ettifaq, but returned to Europe 12 months later when he joined Ajax.

## JORDAN HENDERSON'S AWARDS INCLUDE:

- England U-21 Player of the Year 2012
- Liverpool Young Player of the Year 2011–12
- Sunderland Young Player of the Year 2009–10, 2010–11
- Premier League Goal of the Month September 2016
- England Senior Men's Player of the Year 2019
- FWA Footballer of the Year 2019–20
- Liverpool Fans' Player of the Season 2019–20
- PFA Team of the Year 2019-20

# VIRGIL VAN DIJK

Virgil van Dijk was born on the 8th of July 1991 in Breda, Netherlands and began his professional career at Groningen, before joining Celtic in 2013. He won the Scottish Premiership with Celtic and the League Cup and was named in the PFA Scotland Team of the Year in both his seasons with the Hoops. Having signed for Southampton in 2015, he joined Liverpool in January 2018 for a world record transfer fee of £75 million. As a centre-back for Liverpool and captain of the Netherlands since 2018, making his debut in 2015, Van Dijk's physical strength is renowned.

He is admired for his leadership and aerial skills and widely regarded as one of the world's best defenders. He became the only defender ever to win UEFA Men's Player of the Year award in 2018-19 and, since becoming a Red, the Dutch star has claimed a clean sweep of domestic honours, including two Premier League titles, and helped Liverpool back to the top of European football with the team's Champions League triumph in 2019.

## VIRGIL VAN DIJK'S AWARDS INCLUDE:

- Liverpool Fans Player of the Season Award 2018–19
- Liverpool Players' Player of the Season Award 2018–19
- Southampton Player of the Season 2015–16
- PFA Scotland Team of the Year 2013–14, 2014–15
- Celtic Players' Player of the Year 2013–14
- FIFA Pro World 11 2019, 2020, 2022, 2024
- Football Supporters Federation Player of the Year 2019
- PFA Players' Player of the Year 2018–19
- PFA Team of the Year 2018–19, 2019–20, 2021–22, 2023–24
- UEFA Champions League Team of the Season 2021–22
- Premier League Player of the Season 2018–19
- UEFA Team of the Year 2018, 2019, 2020
- UEFA Men's Player of the Year Award 2018–19

## TRENT JOHN ALEXANDER-ARNOLD

Trent John Alexander-Arnold was born on the 7th of October 1998 in Liverpool. In 2004, he joined Liverpool's academy as a six-year-old, and as a right-back captained the club's youth teams as he rose rapidly through the ranks. His senior debut came in 2016, at the age of 18, and he was in the starting XI for the UEFA Champions League finals in both 2018 and 2019, making him the youngest player in the history of the tournament to start in back-to-back finals.

At international level, the defender made his England debut in 2018 against Costa Rica and became only the fourth teenager to start a match for England in the World Cup in Russia later the same year. Known for his intelligence, impressive passing and accurate crossing, Alexander-Arnold won seven major trophies in his nine seasons of senior football at Anfield, but after 354 first team appearances and 23 goals for his childhood club, he signed for Real Madrid in the summer of 2025.

## TRENT ALEXANDER-ARNOLD'S AWARDS INCLUDE:

- Liverpool Young Player of the Season 2016–17, 2017–18
- Premier League Young Player of the Year 2019–20
- PFA Team of the Year 2018–19, 2019–20, 2021–22
- UEFA Team of the Year 2018–19
- Premier League Player of the Month December 2019, November 2021
- UEFA Champions League Team of the Season 2018–19, 2021–22

## SADIO MANÉ

Sadio Mané was born on the 10th of April 1992 in Sédhiou, Senegal. His professional career took off when he was 19 with French club Metz after which he played for Red Bull Salzburg in Austria and then Southampton in the UK, where his hat-trick, scored in 176 seconds, was the fastest on record. In 2016, the winger was at Liverpool, the fee reported to be £34 million, and helped them win the UEFA Champion's League and the 2019-2020 Premier League.

Mané made his debut for the Senegal national side in 2012 and has scored 19 goals in 69 appearances for them, the fifth all-time top goalscorer.

Unassuming, but able to withstand high pressure, Mané stands out as a complete player whose levels of concentration are second to none. Described as "world class", he has been praised by many for his skill with both feet, his astonishing bursts of speed, wizardry and prolific goalscoring. He is also known for agility, his light touch of the ball, dribbling ability and swift decision-making, besides his brilliant ability to read a game, place a ball and seek out the best position for scoring. His work-rate leaves others in the shade either when attacking or defending.

## SADIO MANÉ'S AWARDS INCLUDE:

- Liverpool Fans Player of the Season Award 2016–17
- Liverpool Players' Player of the Season Award 2016–17
- FIFA FIFA Pro World 11 4th team 2018
- Premier League Golden Boot 2018–19
- UEFA Champions League Squad of the Season 2018–19
- UEFA Team of the Year 2019
- UEFA Champions League Forward of the Season 2018–19 (2nd place)
- AIF African Cup of Nations Team of the Tournament 2019
- African Footballer of the Year 2019
- Onze d'Or 2018–19
- IFFHS Men's World Team 2019

## ANDREW ROBERTSON

Andrew Robertson was born on the 11th of March 1994 in Glasgow. As a left-back, his senior career started at Queen's Park in 2012. He later joined Dundee United and was named SPFA Young Player of the Year for the 2013-14 season. His international debut for Scotland came in 2014 and he is now captain of the team.

By 2014 he was a Hull City player before moving across the country in 2017 to Liverpool in a £8 million deal. Known for his speed, ability to cross accurately and boundless energy, the defender has won eight major trophies with Liverpool, featuring in 69 of the 76 games as the Reds claimed the Premier League title in 2019-20 and again in 2024-25.

### ANDREW ROBERTSON'S AWARDS INCLUDE:

- PFA Scotland Young Player of the Year 2013–14
- PFA Scotland Team of the Year 2013–14
- SPFL Player of the Month November 2013
- SPFL Young Player of the Month September 2013
- PFA Team of the Year 2018–2019, 2019–20
- UEFA Champions League Team of the Season 2021–22
- UEFA Team of the Year 2019

## ALISSON BECKER

Born in Brazil in 1992, the goalkeeper began his professional career with the Internacional club before moving to Europe in 2016 when he signed for Serie A club Roma. Alisson spent two seasons in Italy and joined Liverpool in 2018 for a fee of £67 million, making him the most expensive goalkeeper in history. Since becoming a Red, the South American's reflexes and reliability have made him one of the finest stoppers in European football, and in his seven seasons so far on Merseyside he has clocked up just short of 300 first team appearances.

His first trophy with the club was the Champions League in 2019 and he has since added two Premier League crowns, FA and League Cup wins and the FIFA Club World Cup. First capped by his country in 2015, he featured in both the 2018 and 2022 World Cups and won the Copa América in 2019, hosted by Brazil, after a 3-1 victory over Peru in the final.

## ALISSON BECKER'S AWARDS INCLUDE:

- The Best FIFA Goalkeeper 2019
- The Yashin Trophy 2019
- UEFA Champions League Goalkeeper of the Season 2018–19
- Premier League Golden Glove 2018–19, 2021–22
- UEFA Champions League Squad of the Season 2017–18, 2018–19
- Copa América Golden Glove 2019
- Copa América Team of the Tournament 2019
- UEFA Team of the Year 2019
- PFA Team of the Year 2021–22
- Liverpool Players' Player of the Season 2022–23

# ALEXIS MAC ALLISTER

Born in the city of Santa Rosa in Argentina in 1998, Mac Allister made his name as a youngster with the Argentinos Juniors club before making the move to Europe as a 20-year-old when he signed for Brighton. The midfielder played for four seasons on the South Coast but was lured to Anfield in the summer of 2023 on a five-year deal. In his first two years at Anfield, the star made more than 100 appearances for the Reds and in his first season won the League Cup at Wembley, starting the final against Chelsea, followed by the Premier League title in 2024-25.

At international level, the midfielder became a world champion in 2022 as Argentina triumphed at the World Cup in Qatar. Mac Allister featured in six of his country's seven games, including the victory in the final against France after a penalty shootout, while he claimed another winner's medal in 2024 as Argentina lifted the Copa América for a record-extending 16th time.

## MAC ALLISTER'S AWARDS INCLUDE:

- Premier League Goal of the Month December 2023
- Premier League Player of the Month April 2025
- BBC Goal of the Month December 2023, April 2024, April 2025
- The Athletic Premier League Team of the Season 2024–25

# THE MANAGERS

A BRIEF LIST OF LIVERPOOL MANAGERS

TOM WATSON

## TOM WATSON

Born on the 9th April 1859 and died on the 6th May 1915. He joined Liverpool on the 27th July 1896 and took charge of his first game on the 1st September that year. He took Liverpool on to First Division League title success on two occasions in 1900/01 and 1905/06 and was still in charge in 1914 when Liverpool went to their first FA Cup final, which they lost to Burnley 1-0. Watson was the manager who served the club longest staying with the club for 19 years.

## BILL SHANKLY

Born on the 2nd September 1913 and died on the 29th September 1981. Shankly came to Liverpool in December 1959 and became one of Britain and Liverpool's legendary managers. Liverpool were languishing in the Second Division when he arrived and he began to put together a team that would become one of the best in the First Division.

Shankly worked well with his back room team Bob Paisley and Joe Fagan and by 1962 the club had been promoted to the First Division. Under Shankly's guidance, Liverpool went on to win the League First Division title in 1963/64, 1965/66, and 1972/73. They won the FA Cup in 1964/65 and 1973/74 and the UEFA Cup in 1972/73, the same year that Shankly was awarded Manager of the Year. He became an Officer of the Order of the British Empire in 1974 and was inducted to the English Football Hall of Fame in 2002. He will always be remembered for his famous words, "Some people believe football is a matter of life and death, I am very disappointed with that attitude. I can assure you it is much, much more important than that".

**SHANKLY WORKED WELL WITH HIS BACK ROOM TEAM BOB PAISLEY AND JOE FAGAN.**

## BOB PAISLEY

Bob Paisley was born on the 23rd January 1919 and died on the 14th February 1996. Paisley took over as manager of Liverpool aged 55 when Bill Shankly retired in 1974. He joined Liverpool as a player in May 1939 and retired from playing in 1954 after 253 appearances when he became a physiotherapist for the club and he was one of the original members of the "boot room" which was initiated by Bill Shankly as a place to discuss tactics.

Paisley took over a Liverpool team that had been revitalised by Bill Shankly but his own record was even better and when he was in charge Liverpool dominated English football. He led the team for nine seasons and he brought in at least one trophy for the club in eight of those. Paisley has managed 3 European Cup-winning sides, in 1977, 1978 and 1981. In 2012, this is still a record for any manager. Liverpool then also won the League title 6 times and won 3 league Cups, 5 Charity Shields and one European Super Cup. Paisley received the Manager of the Year award 6 times. By the time Paisley retired in 1983 he had spent 44 years at the club. He then became a club director and right-hand man to Kenny Dalglish when Dalglish became manager.

# THE PRIDE OF ENGLAND!

**Paisley's aces set to conquer Europe . . AGAIN**

## JOE FAGAN

Born on the 12th March 1921 and died on the 30th June 2001 aged 80. He took charge of his first game on 20th August 1983 when Liverpool lost 0-2 against Manchester United in the Charity Shield.

Fagan played centre half with Manchester City and came to Liverpool on June 30th 1958 as a coach. He took over as first team trainer in July 1974 following Bill Shankly's departure, and become Bob Paisley's right-hand man.

As manager of Liverpool, Fagan became the first British football manager to win three major titles in one season claiming the League Cup, the Milk Cup and the European Cup. The Reds were second in the League during both of his years of tenure. Fagan's announcement that he was going to retire came just before Liverpool were about play Juventus in the European Cup final in 1985. Fagan was awarded English Manager of the Year in 1984.

## KENNY DALGLISH

Born on the 4th March 1951 in Glasgow, Scotland, his first game in charge of Liverpool was played on the 17th August 1985 when the Reds beat Arsenal 2-0.

Having agreed to take over the manager position on the condition that Bob Paisley would stay at his side for two years, Dalglish became the first player manager in the English game. He changed the team's style of play and the team continued their winning ways beating Manchester United to the League title and Everton in the FA Cup final.

King Kenny, as he was known amongst Liverpool supporters, managed the club during one of its most successful seasons. He won the League First Division title, the FA Cup twice, the League Cup four times, three European Cups and the UEFA Super Cup.

In 1983 he won the Balloon d'Or Silver Award as well as PFA Player of the Year. He received the FWA Footballer of the Year in 1979 and 1983 and in 2009, Four Four Two named him as the greatest striker in post-war football in Britain. In 2006 he came top of the Liverpool fans' *"100 Players Who Shook the Kop"* poll and he has been inducted into both the English and Scottish Football Halls of Fame.

Dalglish went on to manage Blackburn Rovers, Newcastle United and Celtic before returning to Liverpool for one year in 2011 as caretaker manager.

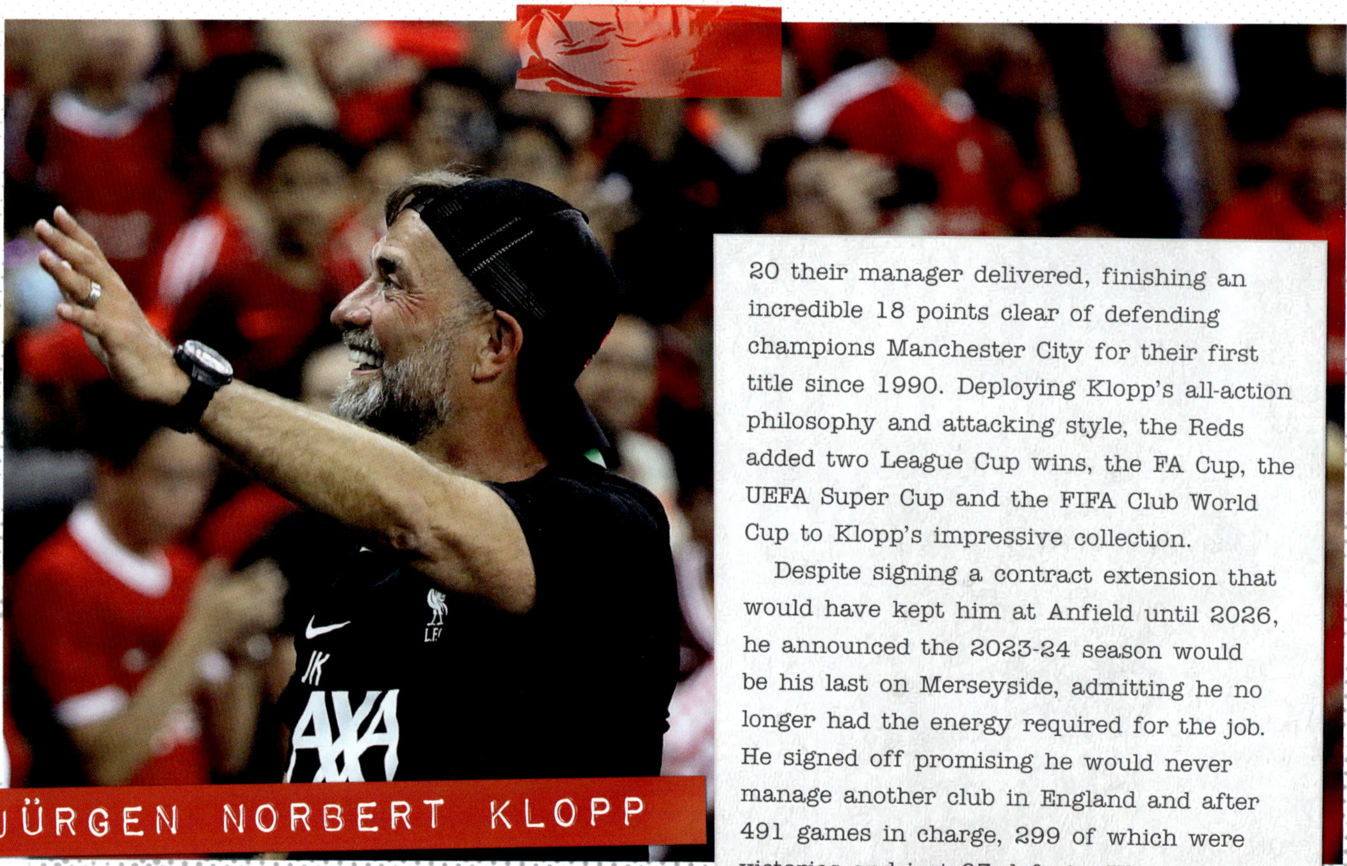

# JÜRGEN NORBERT KLOPP

Born in Stuttgart in 1967, the German began his life as a professional player with 1. FC Pforzheim as a 20-year-old. When he ended his 14-year playing career with Mainz 05, he made the move into coaching with the same team. He stayed with Mainz for seven years, during which his team were promoted to the Bundesliga for the first time in the club's history. He moved on to Borussia Dortmund from 2008 to 2012 and won the DFB-Supercup and back-to-back Bundesliga titles in 2011 and 2012. In October 2015, Klopp joined Liverpool, and in 2016 extended his initial contract by six years. He soon guided the club back into the Champions League and in 2018 their first final in 11 years, which they lost to Real Madrid. Twelve months later the Reds beat Tottenham 2-0 in Klopp's second final and were crowned the champions of Europe for a sixth time, extending the Red's proud record as England's most successful team in the tournament.

Victory was the spark for many more major trophies. Liverpool fans craved Premier League silverware and in 2019-20 their manager delivered, finishing an incredible 18 points clear of defending champions Manchester City for their first title since 1990. Deploying Klopp's all-action philosophy and attacking style, the Reds added two League Cup wins, the FA Cup, the UEFA Super Cup and the FIFA Club World Cup to Klopp's impressive collection.

Despite signing a contract extension that would have kept him at Anfield until 2026, he announced the 2023-24 season would be his last on Merseyside, admitting he no longer had the energy required for the job. He signed off promising he would never manage another club in England and after 491 games in charge, 299 of which were victories and just 83 defeats, Klopp bid an emotional farewell to the Reds.

## JÜRGEN KLOPP'S AWARDS INCLUDE:

- German Football Manager of the Year 2011, 2012, 2019
- Premier League Manager of the Month September 2016, December 2018, March 2019, August 2019, September 2019, November 2019, December 2019, January 2020, May 2021, January 2024
- Onze d'Or Coach of the Year 2019
- World Soccer Awards World Manager of the Year 2019
- Globe Soccer Awards Best Coach of the Year 2019
- League Managers' Association Manager of the Year 2019–20, 2021–22
- Premier League Manager of the Season 2019–20, 2021–22
- The Best FIFA Men's Coach 2019, 2020

## ARNE SLOT

Born in the Netherlands in 1978, Slot enjoyed an 18-year professional career as a midfielder with Dutch sides FC Zwolle, NAC Breda, Sparta Rotterdam and finally PEC Zwolle. He hung up his boots in 2013, at the age of 35, after more than 500 games and 100 goals and began his coaching career. A brief spell with the Cambuur club was followed by his appointment as the manager of top-flight AZ Alkmaar ahead of the 2019-20 season before he was lured away by Dutch giants Feyenoord after just 18 months. He had a massive impact in his three seasons with his new club, leading the team to the Eredivisie title in 2022-23 and the Dutch Cup the following year. Under Slot, Feyenoord also reached the final of the UEFA Conference League in 2022.

His appointment as Liverpool's new manager in the summer of 2024, replacing the popular and hugely successful Jürgen Klopp, was seen by some as a gamble, but Slot's clever tactics and superb man management made him an instant hit on Merseyside. In his first season of Premier League action, his side began strongly and only got better. A single defeat in their first 30 league fixtures sent out a message and after going top of the table in late October, the Reds never surrendered their advantage.

They eventually claimed the title by 10 points ahead of runners-up Arsenal and in the process equalled the record of bitter rivals Manchester United with a 20th English top-flight triumph. In his debut season, Liverpool also reached the League Cup final while victory over Spanish side Girona in the group stages of the Champions League gave the Reds their 150th win in European football. His first year in the Liverpool dugout saw Slot take charge for 56 games in total, of which his team won 38 and were beaten just nine times.

### ARNE SLOT'S AWARDS INCLUDE:

- Rinus Michels Award 2021–22, 2022–23
- LMA Manager of the Year 2024–25
- Premier League Manager of the Season 2024–25
- Premier League Manager of the Month November 2024

**SLOT'S CLEVER TACTICS AND SUPERB MAN MANAGEMENT MADE HIM AN INSTANT HIT ON MERSEYSIDE.**

# THE STATISTICS

## POSITION IN THE LEAGUE:

### DIVISION TWO
1893/94 - 1st

### DIVISION ONE
1894/95 - 16th

### DIVISION TWO
1895/96 - 1st

### DIVISION ONE
1896/97 - 5th
1897/98 - 9th
1898/99 - 2nd
1899/1900 - 10th
1900/01 - 1st
1901/02 - 11th
1902/03 - 5th
1903/04 - 17th

### DIVISION TWO
1904/05 - 1st

### DIVISION ONE
1905/06 - 1st
1906/07 - 15th
1907/08 - 8th
1908/09 - 14th
1909/10 - 2nd
1910/11 - 13th
1911/12 - 15th
1912/13 - 12th
1913/14 - 16th
1914/15 - 13th

### WORLD WAR I

1919/20 - 4th
1920/21 - 4th
1921/22 - 1st
1922/23 - 1st
1923/24 - 12th
1924/25 - 4th
1925/26 - 7th
1926/27 - 9th
1927/28 - 16th
1928/29 - 4th
1929/30 - 12th
1930/31 - 9th
1931/32 - 10th
1932/33 - 14th
1933/34 - 18th
1934/35 - 7th
1935/36 - 19th
1936/37 - 18th
1937/38 - 11th
1938/39 - 11th

### WORLD WAR II

1946/47 - 1st
1947/48 - 11th
1948/49 - 12th
1949/50 - 8th
1950/51 - 9th
1951/52 - 11th
1952/53 - 17th
1953/54 - 22nd

## DIVISION TWO

1954/55 - 11th
1955/56 - 3rd
1956/57 - 3rd
1957/58 - 4th
1958/59 - 4th
1959/60 - 3rd
1960/61 - 3rd
1961/62 - 1st

## DIVISION ONE

1962/63 - 8th
1963/64 - 1st
1964/65 - 7th
1965/66 - 1st
1966/67 - 5th
1967/68 - 3rd
1968/69 - 2nd
1969/70 - 5th
1970/71 - 5th
1971/72 - 3rd
1972/73 - 1st
1973/74 - 2nd
1974/75 - 2nd
1975/76 - 1st
1976/77 - 1st
1977/78 - 2nd
1978/79 - 1st
1979/80 - 1st
1980/81 - 5th
1981/82 - 1st
1982/83 - 1st
1983/84 - 1st
1984/85 - 2nd
1985/86 - 1st
1986/87 - 2nd
1987/88 - 1st
1988/89 - 2nd
1989/90 - 1st
1990/91 - 2nd
1991/92 - 6th

## PREMIER LEAGUE

1992/93 - 6th
1993/94 - 8th
1994/95 - 4th
1995/96 - 3rd
1996/97 - 4th
1997/98 - 3rd
1998/99 - 7th
1999/2000 - 4th
2000/01 - 3rd
2001/02 - 2nd
2002/03 - 5th
2003/04 - 4th
2004/05 - 5th
2005/06 - 3rd
2006/07 - 3rd
2007/08 - 4th
2008/09 - 2nd
2009/10 - 7th
2010/11 - 6th

2011/12 - 8th
2012/13 - 7th
2013/14 - 2nd
2014/15 - 6th
2015/16 - 8th
2016/17 - 4th
2017/18 - 4th
2018/19 - 2nd
2019/20 - 1st
2020/21 - 3rd
2021/22 - 2nd
2022/23 - 5th
2023/24 - 3rd
2024/25 - 1st

# MORE STATS

## CUP COMPETITIONS:

### FA CUP

1914 - Liverpool 0-1 Burnley
1950 - Liverpool 0-2 Arsenal
1965 - Liverpool 2-1 Leeds United
1971 - Liverpool 1-2 Arsenal
1974 - Liverpool 3-0 Newcastle United.
1977 - Liverpool 1-2 Manchester United
1986 - Liverpool 3-1 Everton
1988 - Liverpool 0-1 Wimbledon
1989 - Liverpool 3-2 Everton
1992 - Liverpool 2-0 Sunderland
1996 - Liverpool 0-1 Manchester United
2001 - Liverpool 2-1 Arsenal
2006 - Liverpool 3-3 West Ham United
(Liverpool won 3-1 on penalties)
2012 - Liverpool 1-2 Chelsea
2022 - Liverpool 0-0 Chelsea (a.e.t)
(Liverpool won 6-5 on penalties)

### THE LEAGUE CUP

1978 - Liverpool 0-1 Nottingham Forest
1981 - Liverpool 2-1 West Ham United
1982 - Liverpool 3-1 Tottenham Hotspur
1983 - Liverpool 3-1 Manchester United
1984 - Liverpool 1-0 Everton
1987 - Liverpool 1-2 Arsenal
1995 - Liverpool 2-1 Bolton Wanderers
2001 - Liverpool 1-1 Birmingham City
(Liverpool won on penalties 5-4)
2003 - Liverpool 2-0 Manchester United
2004 - Liverpool 2-3 Chelsea
2012 - Liverpool 2-2 Cardiff City
(Liverpool won on penalties 3-2)
2016 – Liverpool 1-1 Manchester City (a.e.t)
(Manchester won on penalties 3-1)
2022 – Liverpool 0-0 Chelsea (a.e.t)
(Liverpool won on penalties 11-10)
2024 – Liverpool 1-0 Chelsea (a.e.t)
2025 – Liverpool 1-2 Newcastle United

### ENGLISH COMMUNITY SHIELD

2002/03 - Liverpool 0-1 Arsenal
2006/07 - Liverpool 2-1 Chelsea

### ENGLISH SUPER CUP

1986 - Liverpool 7-2 Everton

### ENGLISH CHARITY SHIELD

1922/23 - Liverpool 0-1 Huddersfield Town
1964/65 - Liverpool 2-2 West Ham United (shared)
1965/66 - Liverpool 2-2 Manchester United (shared)
1966/67 - Liverpool 1-0 Everton
1971/72 - Liverpool 0-1 Leicester City

1974/75 - Liverpool 1-1 Leeds United
(Liverpool 16-5 on penalties)
1976/77 - Liverpool 1-0 Southampton
1977/78 - Liverpool 0-0 Manchester United
(shared)
1979/80 - Liverpool 3-1 Arsenal
1980/81 - Liverpool 1-0 West Ham United
1982/83 - Liverpool 1-0 Tottenham Hotspur
1983/84 - Liverpool 0-2 Manchester United
1984/85 - Liverpool 0-1 Everton
1986/87 - Liverpool 1-1 Everton (shared)
1988/89 - Liverpool 2-1 Wimbledon
1989/90 - Liverpool 1-0 Arsenal
1990/91 - Liverpool 1-1 Manchester United (shared)
1992/93 - Liverpool 3-4 Leeds United
2001/02 - Liverpool 2-1 Manchester United

## UEFA CHAMPIONS LEAGUE

2005 - Liverpool 3-3 AC Milan
(Liverpool won 3-2 on penalties)
2007 - Liverpool 1-2 AC Milan
2018 – Liverpool 1-3 Real Madrid
2019 – Liverpool 2-0 Tottenham Hotspur.

## EUROPEAN CUP-WINNERS' CUP

1966 - Liverpool 1-2 Borussia Dortmund

## EUROPEAN CHAMPION'S CUP

1977 - Liverpool 3-1 Borussia Mönchengladbach
1978 - Liverpool 1-0 Club Brugge
1981 - Liverpool 1-0 Real Madrid
1984 - Liverpool 1-1 Roma
(Liverpool won 4-2 on penalties)
1985 - Liverpool 0-1 Juventus

## UEFA SUPER CUP

1978 - Liverpool 7-1 SV Hamburg
1979 - Liverpool 3-4 Anderlecht
1985 - Liverpool 0-2 Juventus
2002 - Liverpool 3-2 Bayern Munich
2006 - Liverpool 3-1 CSKA Moscow
2019 - Liverpool 2-2 Chelsea
(Liverpool won 5-4 on penalties)

## CLUB WORLD CUP 2008

Manchester United 1-0 Liga de Quito

## UEFA EUROPA LEAGUE

2016 - Liverpool 1-3 Seville

## FA COMMUNITY SHIELD

2019/20 - Liverpool 1-1 Manchester City (a.e.t)
(Manchester City won 5-4 on penalties)
2020/21 - Liverpool 1-1 Arsenal (a.e.t)
(Arsenal won on penalties 5-4)
2022/23 - Liverpool 3-1 Manchester City

## FIFA CLUB WORLD CUP

2019 - Liverpool 1-0 Flamengo

YOU'LL NEVER WALK ALONE
Western Union
2019
Standard Chartered
SportPesa